Injustice in Urban Sustainability

T0352802

This book uses a unique typology of ten core drivers of injustice to explore and question common assumptions around what urban sustainability means, how it can be implemented and how it is manifested in or driven by urban interventions that hinge on claims of sustainability.

Aligned with critical environmental justice studies, the book highlights the contradictions of urban sustainability in relation to justice. It argues that urban neighborhoods cannot be greener, more sustainable and livable unless their communities are strengthened by the protection of the right to housing, public space, infrastructure and healthy amenities. Linked to the individual drivers, ten short empirical case studies from across Europe and North America provide a systematic analysis of research, policy and practice conducted under urban sustainability agendas in cities such as Barcelona, Glasgow, Athens, Boston and Montréal and show how social and environmental justice is, or is not, being taken into account. By doing so, the book, its illustrations and its accompanying short videos uncovers the risks of continuing urban sustainability agendas while ignoring, and therefore perpetuating, systemic drivers of inequity and injustice operating within and outside of the city.

Accessibly written for students and scholars in urban studies, critical geography and planning, and critical urban health, this is a useful and analytical synthesis of issues relating to urban sustainability, environmental and social justice.

Panagiota Kotsila is a postdoctoral researcher based at Institute for Environmental Sciences and Technology-Universitat Autònoma de Barcelona (ICTA-UAB) and the Barcelona Lab for Urban Environmental Justice and Sustainability (BCNUEJ).

Isabelle Anguelovski is the director of BCNUEJ, an ICREA research professor, and a principal investigator at ICTA-UAB.

Melissa García-Lamarca is a postdoctoral researcher based at ICTA-UAB and the Barcelona Lab for Urban Environmental Justice and Sustainability (BCNUEJ).

Filka Sekulova is a postdoctoral fellow at Universitat Oberta de Catalunya and an associate researcher at the Barcelona Lab for Urban Environmental Justice and Sustainability (BCNUEJ) and ICTA-UAB.

Routledge Equity, Justice and the Sustainable City
Series editors: Julian Agyeman and Stephen Zavestoski

This series positions equity and justice as central elements of the transition toward sustainable cities. The series introduces critical perspectives and new approaches to the practice and theory of urban planning and policy that ask how the world's cities can become "greener" while becoming more fair, equitable and just.

The *Routledge Equity Justice and the Sustainable City* series addresses sustainable city trends in the global North and South and investigates them for their potential to ensure a transition to urban sustainability that is equitable and just for all. These trends include municipal climate action plans; resource scarcity as tipping points into a vortex of urban dysfunction; inclusive urbanization; "complete streets" as a tool for realizing more "livable cities"; the use of information and analytics toward the creation of "smart cities".

The series welcomes submissions for high-level cutting-edge research books that push thinking about sustainability, cities, justice and equity in new directions by challenging current conceptualizations and developing new ones. The series offers theoretical, methodological, and empirical advances that can be used by professionals and as supplementary reading in courses in urban geography, urban sociology, urban policy, environment and sustainability, development studies, planning, and a wide range of academic disciplines.

Sacred Civics
Building Seven Generation Cities
Edited by Jayne Engle, Julian Agyeman, and Tanya Chung-Tiam-Fook

Injustice in Urban Sustainability
Ten Core Drivers
Panagiota Kotsila, Isabelle Anguelovski, Melissa García-Lamarca and Filka Sekulova

For more information about this series, please visit: www.routledge.com/ Routledge-Equity-Justice-and-the-Sustainable-City-series/book-series/EJSC

Injustice in Urban Sustainability
Ten Core Drivers

Panagiota Kotsila, Isabelle Anguelovski, Melissa García-Lamarca, and Filka Sekulova

Manuscript edits by Ana Cañizares
Illustrations by Carlotta Cataldi

Routledge
Taylor & Francis Group
LONDON AND NEW YORK

from Routledge

First published 2023
by Routledge
4 Park Square, Milton Park, Abingdon, Oxon OX14 4RN

and by Routledge
605 Third Avenue, New York, NY 10158

Routledge is an imprint of the Taylor & Francis Group, an informa business

© 2023 Panagiota Kotsila, Isabelle Anguelovski, Melissa García-Lamarca and Filka Sekulova

British Library Cataloguing-in-Publication Data
A catalogue record for this book is available from the British Library

ISBN: 978-1-032-11762-1 (hbk)
ISBN: 978-1-032-11763-8 (pbk)
ISBN: 978-1-003-22142-5 (ebk)

DOI: 10.4324/9781003221425

Typeset in Times New Roman
by Apex CoVantage, LLC

Contents

Acknowledgments

Rarely does a book of this nature come out of a collaborative European Commission-funded project. Many large research projects funded by schemes such as FP7 or Horizon 2020 do not offer a critical space for collective academic writing on the topic of justice and sustainability—especially not in the form of an academic, open-access book. This book was born from the UrbanA research project, and thanks to the incredibly supportive project team led by Matthew Bach and Lucia Di Paola at ICLEI.

UrbanA was a three-year endeavor in "distilling innovative urban solutions for sustainable and just cities" with partners from Germany, Portugal, Ireland, the UK, the Netherlands, Hungary and Spain. It identified not only best practices in urban sustainability from the Global North (and South, more limitedly) but also drivers of injustice. Too many collaborative research projects tend to focus on solutions, innovations, upscaling and replicability of "best practices" without questioning the key processes, dynamics and actors that shape the relationship between urban sustainability and social injustice. Our partners and the wider UrbanA team entrusted us to unearth and display these drivers of injustice, and for this, we are immensely grateful. We also thank our colleague Prof. James Connolly, who led many of our group's contributions in UrbanA for more than two years and inspired much of the analysis and reflections in this book before moving to the University of British Columbia.

Much of the material presented in this book emerges from our own field work and from the empirical research and analysis conducted by our colleagues in UrbanA, as well as that of the EU projects Naturvation and GreenLULUs. We thank them for their dedication and trust. We are grateful to the members of our Barcelona Lab for Urban Environmental Justice and Sustainability, including the committed interns who contributed their experience and passion toward this writing endeavor. We are particularly thankful to Aaron Vansintjan, Helen Cole, Neil Gray, Francesc Baró, Galia Shokry and Emilia Oscilowicz for their research and insights on, respectively, Montreal, Dallas, Glasgow, Barcelona and Nantes, Boston and Montreal. We also thank our lab colleagues Austin Matheney, Taliah Dommerholt and Jonathan Luger, who contributed to the meta-analysis of EU projects around sustainability and justice.

We deeply thank our manuscript editor Ana Cañizares, who closely followed this work from its early stages, offering developmental editing, line-editing, copyediting and proofreading, and ensuring that the book was academically sharp and concise in its messages. Thank you also to Carlotta Cataldi for her work on graphically visualizing some of the core ideas in our research and to Kapala Studios for filming our short illustrative videos.

As field researchers, the four of us are also eternally grateful to the community groups, organizers, neighborhood leaders, planners, elected officials and other urban stakeholders who we engaged with and interviewed over the years in cities as diverse as Barcelona, Dublin, Glasgow, Manchester, Nantes, Athens, Sofia, Montreal, Boston, Philadelphia and Washington DC. We deeply thank the people who followed our work with UrbanA for three years sharing their challenges and insights, and who today form a community of practice around sustainable and just cities.

Our time, effort and multiple rounds of field work were supported and funded by different fellowships, grants and EU projects. These include funding from the European Union's Horizon 2020 research and innovation program under URBANA (GA822357), GREENLULUS (GA678034), NATURVATION (GA730243) and WEGO-ITN (GA764908). It also received the support of the Spanish Ministry of Science through the Juan de la Cierva (IJC2019–040934-I, IJC2020–046064-I) and the Maria de Maeztu (CEX2019–000940-M) schemes as well as the ICREA research professorship program. We would not have been able to extensively research justice and sustainability without this core support throughout the years. Thank you also to Julian Agyeman, Stephen Zavestovski and our team of Routledge colleagues for believing in this project.

Last, we would like to thank the broader community of the Institute of Environmental Science and Technology (ICTA) at the Universitat Autònoma de Barcelona for creating an incredibly stimulating, critical and caring research environment. We owe you our daily survival in academia! And of course, this book would have never seen the light of day without the support of our partners, families and the unstoppable small humans in our lives (Alan, Leonidas, Diego, Júlia, Hristo, Albena, Chris, Deia and Manon), who gifted us with the motivation and space to focus on such a meaningful project.

To all of you, thank you.

Introduction

Urban sustainability beyond techno-political fixes: an exploration of ten core drivers of injustice

In spring 2019, before the COVID-19 pandemic had become a global reality, the European-funded project UrbanA[1] began engaging a community of practice around issues of urban sustainability and justice by bringing together research and community partners across seven countries in Europe. In our first encounter, academics, policymakers, local government representatives, non-profit organizations and activists came across some of the challenges around designing and implementing urban sustainability with the notion of justice at its core. Among other themes, participants discussed socially just and ecologically sound ways of renaturing cities that involve protecting the right to housing, urban nature and healthy environments and preventing the often-contradictory effects of such objectives, such as green gentrification. We explored the potential repercussions of a more feminist and care-centered approach to planning for urban sustainability that would recognize and center the undervalued, gendered and often invisibilized work of care (for people and nature). We also debated how to achieve socioecological justice through processes of urban commoning, movement organizing, creating, and supporting solidarity networks, and maintaining the social fabric that makes urban communities more cohesive and resilient.

Nevertheless, as motivated and well-intentioned as these discussions were, they could not avoid contradiction. Embedded in a highly privileged environment with an educated and intellectual crowd of professionals, the majority of those with decision-making power were Western, white and male. As we were offered mint tea prepared by an undoubtedly empowered collective of women cooks of African origin who had started their small business in a northern European city at a venue dedicated to the heritage of immigration in that city, we could not help but notice the contradictions around us: right across the street, bulldozers paved the way for an urban regeneration project known to be displacing long-term residents including immigrant minorities from the neighborhood. It was during these

DOI: 10.4324/9781003221425-1

uncomfortable moments that the concept of "urban sustainability and justice" manifested itself as a complex system of power and privilege that can only be addressed through a deeper engagement with on-the-ground realities and our own positionality and responsibility toward them. This book draws on these reflections to analyze ten drivers of urban injustice and how they are being challenged and transformed.

Situating urban sustainability

Nearly three decades after the Rio Declaration and Local Agenda 21, urban sustainability goals are still deeply challenged by rapidly unfolding climate change impacts, growing geopolitical conflicts and the tandem economic and public health crises. In 2013, UNESCO's World Social Science Report emphasized the need to address environmental change as interconnected with a multitude of other risks, crises and vulnerabilities. "The social, economic and environmental dimensions of sustainable development are a single agenda", it proclaimed (ISSC/UNESCO 2013). Nearly ten years later, in the most recent World Social Report (UNDESA 2020), urbanization is listed as one of four megatrends facing humanity, along with climate change, technological innovation and international migration. The report concludes that cities globally are characterized by inequality and that underserved urban neighborhoods continue to be exposed to concentrated poverty, which leads to further socioeconomic marginalization and exclusion in conjunction with accelerating environmental degradation (Ibid.).

Linking urban sustainability and climate change, the latest IPCC report (IPCC 2022), and specifically Chapter 6, confirms the centrality of cities for climate change impacts and action, in relation both to the increasing hazard risks faced by urban areas and to their strategic potential to carry out combined adaptation and mitigation actions whose benefits for broader urban sustainability and justice goals can have global repercussions (Dodman et al. 2022, 113). While low- and middle-income nations and smaller and medium-sized urban centers are, comparably, more vulnerable to climate risks, climate impacts are also disproportionately felt by the most economically and socially marginalized communities within larger cities and higher-income nations. More importantly, efforts to respond to such unequal risks through policies and interventions that aim to strengthen adaptation, resilience or sustainability, often exacerbate inequality by shifting risks from one community to the other, leaving core social issues unaddressed or creating new problems that continue to impact the most vulnerable (Ibid.). The report stresses with high confidence that a focus on justice by prioritizing climate risk reduction for low-income and marginalized residents can bring the greatest gains in terms of well-being for urban areas. Yet none of those goals are likely to be achieved without addressing historical and structural inequality, poverty and segregation while safeguarding general health and well-being for all. The purpose of this book is to elaborate on a clear set of factors—ten key drivers of injustice operating in the context of urban societies—that must be addressed for cities to tackle these issues in a meaningful way.

While the problems faced by cities today are more linked to the climate emergency than when urban sustainability was first articulated, sustainability is nonetheless a relevant and powerful concept that embraces the complexity of socioenvironmental systems and considers the well-being of present and future generations. Though concepts such as "climate change resilience" or "climate emergency responses" have taken precedence, sustainability continues to underpin much of urban planning practice, policymaking and global agendas. In the UN Agenda 2030 for Sustainable Development (2015), cities and urban development have become a standalone goal (SDG 11), which includes objectives for inclusivity, safety, resilience and sustainability. Increasingly, then, city governments are making some version of sustainability an explicit policy goal, materializing in a wide range of policies and interventions such as green corridors, cycling lanes, digital fabrication, clean energy production, community gardens, co-living schemes, sustainable housing, food sharing or nature-based solutions, to name a few. Navigating such compounded and complex objectives, moving beyond sustainability as an empty signifier and toward its genuine implementation, and dealing with the many contradictions and trade-offs involved in this process, is the multifaceted challenge cities face today. At its core, it is a question of how to make sustainability more than just a techno-political fix (McCarthy 2015).

The double contradiction of urban sustainability

Demands for bringing the equity-oriented principles and approaches of environmental justice into sustainability policies have been echoing for more than 20 years (Agyeman, Bullard, and Evans 2002), yet interventions integrating sustainability and justice remain as urgent as ever, especially so in cities. Like sustainable development, urban sustainability carries the promise of a "green, profitable, and fair" future with compatible economic, environmental and social goals. Though the social dimensions of sustainability are on occasion framed in terms of equity or justice, they are often the least priority, or the "short leg" supporting the urban sustainability stool in public policy; they are "named but not fully explored or addressed" (Pearsall and Pierce 2010). Cities such as Vancouver, Amsterdam, Copenhagen and Nantes, for example, compete with one another for the title of the most sustainable city, articulating a visibly green brand to attract investors and upper-class residents, but exhibit little in the way of equity and inclusivity. Most sustainability agendas that prioritize economic "green" performance often leave questions of justice behind (Garcia-Lamarca et al. 2021; Anguelovski and Connolly 2021).

Central to our analysis is that discourses and practices around sustainability present integral contradictions and that sustainability is not politically neutral. It is crucial here to discern between the "weak" and "strong" versions of sustainability. While weak sustainability, as laid down in the foundational Brundtland report of 1987, is premised upon the notion that continuous economic growth can integrate and even enhance environmental protection, from a strong sustainability standpoint this assumption is unfounded, irrelevant and dangerous (Bonnedahl, Heikkurinen, and Paavola 2022). Policies based on strong sustainability are radically different in terms of their social inclusiveness and the need to respect nature beyond its potential usefulness (Ibid.). As critical scholars have emphasized, weak sustainability discourses are constructed on the supposition that continuous economic growth is compatible with climate change mitigation, lowering global CO_2 emissions, biodiversity loss and maintaining the stability of Earth systems. Evidence, however, unequivocally points out that economic growth and strong sustainability grow in opposite directions (Haberl et al. 2020). In terms of both emissions and broader patterns of environmental damage, mainstream liberal articulations of (weak) sustainability seek to balance or counteract ecological degradation without openly questioning the socioeconomic systems that sustain it and that are embedded in unequal relations of power. A strong sustainability agenda, instead, places economic activity at the service of humans and other life on the planet, focusing on serving basic needs and global equity, rather than demand and efficiency (Bonnedahl, Heikkurinen, and Paavola 2022).

The second core contradiction concerns the negative effects produced indirectly or inadvertently through apparently beneficial goods such as urban greening projects and climate adaptation interventions. Critical scholarship from urban studies, geography and broader social sciences, particularly in the context of the United States, has provided ample analysis of how urban sustainability and environmentalism must confront their intersectional blindness to social inequality (Caniglia, Vallée, and Frank 2016; Pellow 2016). Scholars have noted, for example, how making neighborhoods more climate resilient can generate gentrification and push out vulnerable residents—mostly working class, immigrants and people of color—thus "remaking the city for the sustainability class" (Gould and Lewis 2016) living in green resilient enclaves, such as in Philadelphia, Boston, and increasingly so in European cities such as Copenhagen or Barcelona (Anguelovski and Connolly 2021). Such uneven and excluding urban intensification and regeneration (see Chapter 3) can not only lead to increasing housing prices and displacement but also have profound effects on the physical and mental health of those residents who manage to stay, disrupting their sense of place and cohesion (Valli 2015), changing the character and prices of local businesses or hindering access to healthy and affordable food (Alkon and Cadji 2020). These impacts are further exacerbated when processes of urban change happen without the meaningful and inclusive participation of citizens, especially those in vulnerable, marginalized and underinvested neighborhoods (see Chapter 9).

Colonialism and racial capitalism are the foundational historic social relations that underpin this unequal distribution of environmental "goods and bads", profoundly shaping the urban space as well as how and why the city is remade for the so-called sustainability class. What we describe as racialized or ethnically exclusionary urbanization (see Chapter 2) concerns urban development processes and outcomes that ignore, dismiss or discount the experiences of non-white or non-European working-class residents. We dedicate special attention to this process due to its centrality in driving urban injustice. As an alternative, scholars and activists have most recently called for effective justice-oriented solutions that abolish the foundational and systemic violence of society (Pulido and De Lara 2018), proposals that we also explore in this book.

How neoliberalism shaped sustainability

Certainly, the two contradictions of urban sustainability are not unrelated. The emergence of sustainability discourse in the 1970s and early 1980s aligned with the mainstreaming and expansion of another set of ideas and practices in the West and beyond—that of neoliberalism. Neoliberal ideology proposes that society should function based on competition, within "an institutional framework characterized by strong private property rights, free markets and free trade", whereby individuals can compete against each other according to their "entrepreneurial freedoms and skills" (Harvey 2007, 2). This includes the marketization and deregulation of previously publicly run services and provisions ("rollback" of the state), as well as the re-regulation and adoption of profit- and efficiency-oriented logics within public institutions ("roll-out" of the state) (Peck and Tickell 2002). Weak sustainability and neoliberalism have been and continue to be two parallel and porous processes evident in most initiatives claiming to promote "green growth" or similar discourses, linking and consolidating contradictions of social equity and of economic versus ecological benefits in sustainability (see Chapter 10). As Castán Broto and Westman (2019, 214) emphasize, "a remaining barrier to the widespread incorporation of social well-being into sustainability initiatives is this emphasis on technology innovation, eco-efficiency and green growth, which constructs sustainability as a fortuitous investment agenda".

Examples of such processes in cities can be found in interventions that privatize or commodify nature in the name of sustainability and at the expense of vulnerable minorities and marginalized groups through uneven and excluding urban intensification and regeneration (see Chapter 3). Much criticism from academia and beyond has been directed, for example, at the conversion of former industrial land and infrastructure into lush greenways, such as the 606 in Chicago, the BeltLine in Atlanta and the High Line in New York, which tend to be surrounded by high-end real estate developments. These exclusionary dynamics are also enacted as part of transit-oriented developments and their associated increased housing prices, in cities such as Portland, Denver, Copenhagen or Boston (Gould and Lewis 2016; Immergluck and Balan 2018; see also Chapter 5).

Social equity is also compromised when neoliberal principles push a process that has been described as the "NGO-ization" of sustainability (Argüelles 2021b), placing the responsibility to enact sustainability outside the welfare state and into the hands of non-governmental organizations (NGOs), volunteers, community groups and citizens. While an active presence of civil society is linked to stronger and more just sustainability outcomes (see Chapter 8), it is also the case that "sharing" sustainability decision-making and action with actors outside the state (private, social or civil) may lead to weaker impacts, exclusive reach and the stretching thin of already vulnerable individuals, groups and non-profits—in other words, depoliticizing urban governance (see Chapter 7). In Bristol, for example, austerity policies have undermined the ability of the parks department to adequately protect and maintain green space, with deeper impacts experienced by historically marginalized neighborhoods such as South Bristol, where many civic groups are forced to take over such responsibilities (Matheney, del Pulgar, and Shokry 2021).

How then can cities become more inclusive and just, while also responding to the current climate and health emergencies and the multiple socioenvironmental challenges that already beset urban residents worldwide? How and why do sustainability initiatives that set out to address socioenvironmental justice often end up compromising it? The answers are neither straightforward nor simple, and this book does not claim to provide all of them. However, we believe that to move toward urban sustainability that promotes social and environmental justice, we must first understand the historical and ongoing processes that perpetuate injustice in the current context of urban sustainability efforts. In other words, we must look at the factors that contribute to the misalignment of sustainability initiatives with objectives of social justice, redistribution, emancipation and equal opportunity.

We join the call of critical scholars who urge for urban sustainability to move away from monolithic economic assessments of progress and apolitical understandings of ecology, challenging planning orthodoxies that praise "Smart Sustainable Resilient City" paradigms (Connolly 2019). Instead, we advocate a true integration of social justice and sustainability, defined as "the need to ensure a better quality of life for all, now and into the future, in a just and equitable manner, whilst living within the limits of supporting ecosystems" (Agyeman, Bullard, and Evans 2003, 5). In line with critical environmental justice studies, and drawing from fields such as political ecology, urban environmental justice, critical race, gender and feminist theory, we argue that urban neighborhoods cannot be more environmentally sustainable and livable unless their communities are strengthened via the protection of their rights to housing, land, public space, healthy amenities and urban nature (see Chapters 2 and 5). Efforts toward socially and environmentally just sustainabilities would thus need to consider the relationships between urban space, social power and different overlapping identities, subjectivities and vulnerabilities.

Articulating drivers of injustice in urban sustainability

In creating a unique typology of ten core drivers of injustice (including distributive, procedural, recognition and epistemic injustice), we analyze the conditions concerned with the distribution of resources, the political processes and the differential social recognition that systematically support some but hinder others from achieving what they value in order to live a healthy and fulfilled life within reasonable limits (Fraser 2005; Nussbaum 2000; Schlosberg 2013). We specifically examine the way these conditions relate to how urban sustainability is conceptualized, implemented and experienced.

By problematizing the apparently benign or politically "neutral" nature of sustainability, we question the common assumptions around what urban sustainability means to different people and address the risk of continuing to practice urban sustainability in a way that ignores, and thus perpetuates, structures of urban injustice operating at institutional, systemic and intimate levels. In light of the current economic, climate and public health crises, now deepened by the devastating war in Ukraine, we believe a diagnosis of this kind is essential for guiding informed responses from academics, practitioners and grassroots organizations. Rather than adhering blindly to mainstream visions of urban sustainability, we argue that it is essential to uncover the enduring and often-overlooked drivers that prevent the realization of just sustainabilities.

Each of the following ten chapters is a thick description of one of the ten drivers, highlighting the underlying and ongoing injustices experienced by vulnerable or marginalized groups by way of sustainability efforts. This is done by combining a comparative and international analysis of such phenomena in various cities, including in-depth case study vignettes from the Global North. Our textual analysis can be complemented by viewing a series of ten short videos which offer a quick introduction to each of the chapters that follow. Additionally, the material presented in this book is accompanied by online StoryMaps platforms with mini documentaries for many of the case studies and vignettes (e.g., Washington DC, Boston, Nantes, Portland, Montreal, Boston and Barcelona).[2]

This book builds on individual and collaborative research on urban justice and sustainability and a systematic and comprehensive analysis of critical research conducted in the last decade, mostly in the EU and North America, pertaining to themes like urban greening, nature-based solutions, sustainable mobility, sustainable food systems, waste management and circular economy, clean energy, and climate adaptation. This research was conducted under the framework of large scale, mostly comparative and international research projects in which we took part, mostly between 2011 and 2022 (i.e., the European FP7 and H2020 projects UrbLiv, ENTITLE, TESS, Naturvation, GreenLULUs and UrbanA) and dozens of others we report on, including AGAPE, EditCitNet, NATURE4CITIES, SHARE-CITY and more. We also draw on global literature from urban planning, urban and environmental governance, critical geography, degrowth and urban and environmental sociology, to contextualize evidence, findings and claims more broadly.

As scholars from the Global North, we acknowledge the imbalance of geographical representation—particularly in the city case studies—presented in this book. This reflects our own research experience and does not intend to insinuate that sustainable and just urbanism is mostly a question grappled with, explored or performed in Global North cities. Whenever possible, we have provided emblematic and critical examples of how the ten drivers of injustice also operate in the context of cities in the Global South. We acknowledge and engage with the epistemological biases in urban sustainability more broadly, including power-knowledge asymmetries that we address as a driver of injustice (see Chapter 9).

Finally, although we base our analysis of justice and sustainability in this book on cities, the politics and contradictions of urban sustainability are not contained within city limits. The term "planetary urbanization" or the global "social metabolism" of cities refers to how urbanization processes are sustained by resources, materials and waste that is, respectively, extracted from, or shifted *elsewhere*, hence affecting "othered" bodies and subjectivities. In this sense, our research explores how unequal urbanization and the global economic growth imperative produce socioecological impacts and injustices well beyond one single city, region or country (see Chapter 10).

Aware of the need for engaging analysis that can be easily grasped by students, scholars, activists, planners and other professionals, we intend for this book to have a broad reach beyond academia. We hope to prompt numerous reflections and conversations among stakeholders working at the intersection of sustainability and justice and to trigger new research and activism on the topic.

Notes

1 https://urban-arena.eu/
2 See the Resources tab at www.bcnuej.org or follow the QR code offered in the last section of this book.

MATERIAL & LIVELIHOOD INEQUALITIES

Figure 1 Driver 1: Material and Livelihood Inequalities

1 Driver 1

Material and livelihood inequalities

Material and livelihood inequalities (Figure 1) as a driver of injustice in urban sustainability concern the underlying unequal distribution of economic resources and how they reinforce and exacerbate unjust outcomes. It refers to the differential access to economic (i.e., credit, wages, income and financial) assets and other resources (i.e., nature, infrastructure and social networks), as well as the unequal access to means of making a living (i.e., education, specific capabilities, skills, assets, activities, knowledge and information). Such inequalities are historically drawn and perpetuated along lines of class, race, gender, ethnicity, sexuality, religion and their intersections. They can manifest as the unequal distribution of goods and burdens in each society, or between geographically distant places and groups. In this sense, we see material and livelihood inequalities as both a driver and an expression of injustice, with historical processes of oppression and marginalization created by—and in turn maintaining—relations of power and deep divides.

Defining a just level of well-being constitutes a debate in society over what is "necessary" and how much is "enough" to secure a healthy and satisfying life within a framework of sustainability and justice. These questions can only be answered when contextualized, historicized and politicized, and it is not our purpose here to define universal metrics and thresholds of well-being or decent living. Rather, we aim to demonstrate how structurally unequal access to material resources and means of livelihood impacts people's opportunities to experience lives they have a reason to value. Our positioning is closely related to Amartya Sen's capability approach, which highlights the importance of individuals gaining real freedoms and opportunities needed to thrive as communities living in specific contexts. These include access to necessities like food and shelter as well as social needs such as a sense of belonging or place attachment (Sen 2000). Martha Nussbaum further argues for the fulfillment of the conditions that

DOI: 10.4324/9781003221425-2

can help achieve what she calls "central capabilities", or the "basic social minimum" of capabilities in order to achieve human dignity (Nussbaum 2006, 70). We examine the lack of these conditions as a driver of injustice in how it shapes the differential access to and impacts of various urban sustainability interventions such as new green spaces, bicycle lanes or food cooperatives.

Groups facing material inequalities have thus often experienced various forms of exclusion, discrimination, and violence in urban environments, some more slow, embodied and invisible while others more obvious, sensational and documented (Truelove and Ruszczyk 2022). In a context of neoliberal urban governance with increasingly privatized and underregulated housing/rental markets and limited protective social welfare nets, abrupt urban regeneration with strong sustainability claims can, for example, lead to residential displacement and undermine the supposed trickle-down effects of sustainability. This is clearly demonstrated by the phenomenon of green (or eco-, climate, environmental) gentrification (Shokry, Connolly, and Anguelovski 2020), whereby greening or environmental interventions that were intended to improve environmental conditions in neighborhoods end up "generating (or enhancing) gentrification that pushes out the working class, and people of colour [. . .] remaking the city for the sustainability class" (Gould and Lewis 2016). Exclusion and the production of inequality in the context of sustainability can also take more subtle forms. In Swedish cities, the "digital gap" is impacting access to smart public transportation services. While smartphone usage to buy online tickets reduces the use of printed tickets, it also risks excluding those who do not have access to this technology (van Ryneveld 2021). Excluding these realities and accounts from the process of planning is bound to reproduce exclusionary urban visions of sustainability. Not recognizing—and thus failing to address—pre-existing material and intersectional inequalities when designing for sustainability is one form of reproducing injustice, further challenging the potential of vulnerable residents to benefit from resulting interventions.

Accessible and just urban sustainability is thus challenged by material inequalities both through sustainability's direct links to economic power and through indirect links that have to do with civic rights and participation in public dialogue. Material inequalities link together and foreground several other drivers of injustice in the context of urban sustainability presented in this book. As the following chapters unfold in greater detail, low-income and minority or racialized populations are examples of collectives often excluded from urban sustainability and its benefits, due to long-standing oppression and marginalization that intersect with inequalities along lines of gender, age, sexuality or dis/ability, to name a few. Here we examine two core issues related to material and livelihood inequalities as a driver of injustice in the context of urban sustainability: (1) low-wage jobs, as an expression of persistent income inequalities generating intergenerational and racial/ethnic wealth gaps that limit the efficacy of urban sustainability programs, manifested in mobility, food and energy infrastructures, and (2) unaffordable housing, as a condition that limits the efficacy of urban sustainability initiatives.

Low-wage jobs and low incomes

Low-wage jobs, generally referring to jobs that pay less than two-thirds of the national median or mean of gross hourly wages, make up an important part of economies worldwide. In the United States, for example, 25% of all jobs are low-wage, and mobility to better-paid jobs has significantly reduced since the late 1990s (Mosthaf, Schank, and Schnabel 2014). Urban residents with low wages and no alternative income sources struggle to make ends meet. The so-called income gap, meaning the stark difference between the income levels of different groups, is especially pronounced between the lowest earning and highest earning groups in cities. This is related to and reflected on the urban territory through socioeconomic segregation (Tammaru et al. 2020). As found by a detailed study of 24 cities across the world, the richest residents tend to concentrate in city centers and coastal regions, while the poorest concentrate in urban/peri-urban edges, with the residential choices of the top socioeconomic groups driving changes in the geography of segregation (van Ham et al. 2021). In a country like the United States, low wages only increase the already abysmal intergenerational interracial wealth cap, which is illustrated by the fact that in 2017 median white families were projected to own 86 times more wealth than Black families in the following four years (Asante-Muhammad et al. 2017).

These dynamics of inequality perpetuate in time if no action is taken to reverse them. Higher-income neighborhoods, for example, have economically prospered over the last 20 years, while lower-income ones have stagnated or lost economic power (Bailey, van Gent, and Musterd 2017). Classic environmental justice studies show how this perpetuation is expressed in the differential access to environmental goods and benefits (such as clean water and fresh healthy food) or to burdens of unwanted "externalities" (such as toxic waste or air pollution), to which the poorest, racialized and most marginalized and underserved populations are most exposed (Pulido 2008). In a similar way, low wages, unemployment and difficulty in accessing the job market can perpetuate inequalities and limit access to urban sustainability initiatives and their benefits. In the case of retrofitted housing, for example, it is income inequalities and low wages that often preclude the affordability or access to improvements in energy efficiency or renewable sources. Although subsidies exist in some cities to incentivize retrofitting, low-income residents who rent and suffer from fuel poverty are unable to afford the upfront costs for such improvements, while their landlords are not incentivized enough (Camprubí et al. 2016). Moreover, amidst a climate of housing instability where occupants must continually relocate due to gentrification, the prospect of investment in retrofitting is not an attractive one, even if it is the most economic option in the long term. As the following chapters discuss, exclusive access to urban sustainability initiatives and their benefits can be the result of both decisions on the placement of sustainability interventions (prioritizing already affluent and privileged neighborhoods) and the ways in which those interventions are designed, implemented or accessed (excluding the most marginalized).

Different kinds of material inequalities intersect in time and space to produce injustice (distributional, procedural, epistemic and representational, among others). An emerging insight is, for example, that high levels of income inequality in an area result in lower citizen participation, creating negative loops of injustice.[1] The complexity and co-dependency are also well exemplified in the case of *eco-cities*—once a radical concept that emerged from urban ecology thinking—that has taken hold in China over the last decade. Neo and Pow (2015) note how eco-cities in China are often situated in areas undergoing rapid economic development and established through state-business alliances. Both the placement and the decision-making processes around eco-cities are contested in terms of the injustice inflicted upon populations who end up being displaced due to such new eco-developments. Research shows how the development of what turned out to be considered an emblematic eco-city in Tianjin, China, was enabled through the provision of grants and tax breaks to large companies willing to participate in its development, part of the global urban boosterism and green entrepreneurialism wave (Caprotti, Springer, and Harmer 2015). Research on the same site showed how commercial interests were favored over ecological concerns such as bird conservation efforts when the eco-city expanded toward the seaside wetlands and salt marshes (Toxopeus et al. 2020). At the same time, social housing percentage was reduced from 50 to 20% to decrease overall costs, after it forced 2,000 residents to relocate under questionable compensation processes (Ibid.).

Unaffordable housing

The cost of securing safe housing can be prohibitive, especially for people in the lowest income ranks. In a context of reduced social and public housing funding during the last decade of neoliberal austerity, many working-class and low-wage residents find themselves overworking and barely able to pay the bills. In the EU, for example, the share of the urban population living in a household where total housing costs represent more than 40% of disposable income in 2019 was 11.8% (EUROSTAT 2021) while on average 20.0% of disposable income was dedicated to housing costs in the same year (Ibid.). Housing affordability is also diminished as it becomes increasingly financialized, meaning that its value as an asset to invest and speculate with is greater than its use value as a home. Housing financialization shapes inequalities in cities and exacerbates challenges for sustainability, demonstrated by efforts to implement nature-based solutions such as "edible city" ideas (Säumel, Reddy, and Wachtel 2019; Sekulova et al. 2021a).

Unaffordable housing has thus proven central to the social struggles contained within urban sustainability initiatives. Research in real estate economics has indicated time and again that the creation of parks, bike lanes, sustainable housing or even urban gardens enhances the desirability of a neighborhood—sometimes even before these are developed—contributing to an increase in property values and of investments in luxury homes. In the United States, this has been observed in Brooklyn Beach Park New York and in the Atlanta BeltLine (Gould and Lewis 2016; Immergluck 2009), among others. Unregulated market prices in the sector often result in the gentrification of the most attractive green and sustainable neighborhoods, making them exclusive to elites and displacing more vulnerable, long-term residents. In Atlanta, for example, the creation of the BeltLine increased the value of nearby homes up to 26.6% more than houses elsewhere in the region (Immergluck and Balan 2018).

It is common that environmental and housing inequalities intersect to create injustice in cities, challenging the health and well-being of the most vulnerable residents. In The Liberties, a historic, postindustrial and densely populated working-class neighborhood in Dublin, Ireland, residents face a very low rate of access to green space and a severe shortage of affordable housing. In recent years, The Parks Department of the Dublin City Council showed interest in increasing access to green spaces in the neighborhood and released The Liberties Greening Strategy in 2015 (Dublin City Council 2015). However, the implementation of this non-binding proposal has been at odds with the City's housing development plans due to limited land availability in the area. Consequently, intercouncil departmental interests often clash. A temporary halt in investments and construction of real estate developments after the 2008 financial crisis, in combination with strong grassroots mobilizations for more public green spaces for play and recreation, pushed for the creation of new neighborhood parks on municipal land that remained vacant. However, and despite the communal benefits that this new greening has brought, the promotion of The Liberties as a new central green neighborhood with tourist attractions has also led to the rapid rise of rental prices and high-end construction, in turn leading to an acceleration of gentrification and the ensuing displacement of residents (Anguelovski et al. 2021b).

Investment interests and the development of new elite neighborhoods often go hand in hand with the further deterioration of low-class marginalized ones that do not harness equal economic and political attention, becoming more and more neglected by authorities. Research has shown, for example, that across the United States, climate change disproportionately affects Black communities, exacerbating their social vulnerabilities. In the Black Belt, Georgia, a group of counties where at least 40% of the population identifies as Black or African American, housing and property adaptation to extreme climate impacts was found to be economically prohibitive, possibly leading to home and property loss (Iacovino, Stevens, and Song 2021). Political ecologist Timothy Collins (2010) further describes such processes of facilitation and marginalization, whereby powerful geographical groups are enabled to minimize negative environmental impacts and appropriate the benefits, while less powerful groups are unequally exposed to risk. Through his study of a flood disaster, he exposes how socially disparate flood-prone landscapes are produced between the North (USA) and the South (Mexico), and within each city, with privileged areas in Ciudad Juarez representing "the North of the South", and marginalized areas of El Paso representing the "South in the North".

Unaffordable housing and real estate speculation also diminish the possibility of grassroots and/or civil society-led and self-funded sustainability projects to emerge and thrive in urban and peri-urban environments (see also Driver 7). In the case of small-scale organic farmers, for example, who struggle to compete with a globalized and unsustainable food market, real estate speculation and the gentrification of peri-urban areas (a phenomenon intensified by the COVID-19 pandemic) make securing affordable land for cultivation even more difficult. These constraints limit both the farmers' livelihoods and accessibility to fresh, locally produced and organic food for urban residents (Säumel, Reddy, and Wachtel 2019).

Grassroots action and policy tools

Some of the policies that could address material and livelihood inequalities, especially in the context of urban sustainability, would be as overarching as the establishment of a universal basic income and a fairer taxation system and redistribution of wealth in society. This can be thought of as a global approach to redistribute wealth by reducing fees on international remittances, a direct global tax and indirect taxation to finance universal benefits for poorer countries and vulnerable groups, and toward mitigating global environmental degradation and climate change (Borowy 2019). A core aspect advocated by feminists is also a basic care income and its articulation within environmental goals and policies such as the Green New Deal (Adler, Wargan, and Prakash 2019, 35).

Measures directly related to urban planning and regulation include inclusionary zoning—a measure that has to do with regulating land use, often by municipalities, affecting the activity of developers. Inclusionary zoning establishes the obligation for new developments to include affordable housing units to prevent segregation in mixed communities and enable lower-income groups to access new beneficial (green) amenities without any extra public spending. Another anti-gentrification and anti-displacement policy is to control the number of tourist and short-term rental apartments. In cities that attract a large number of tourists throughout the year, residents are displaced due to rising values of properties and rents, and, in some cases, neighborhoods become unaffordable for any future long-term tenants as they are completely taken over by tourists (Cocola-Gant and Lopez-Gay 2020). Some municipal governments have taken measures to control or reverse this situation by prohibiting short-term rentals in certain overburdened neighborhoods, applying limits to AirBnB rentals, limiting the rental period to tourists (e.g., in Barcelona, no rental without a license for a period of less than or equal to 31 days), and increased taxation.

In terms of increasing access to sustainable alternatives, a promising approach is to provide basic income allowances (Laín, Riutort, and Julià 2019), grants and possibly subsidized loans in order for low-income groups to be able to carry out energy efficiency improvements or even simply afford paying rent. In one example of an implemented retrofitting policy in London, over 50,000 homes were retrofitted via the London Warm Zone program and the independent charity National Energy Action (Lewis, Hógáin, and Borghi 2013, 26). However, it has been found that retrofitting itself can be a driver of displacement as well, as real estate prices increase and low-income residents can no longer pay the rent (Bouzarovski, Frankowski, and Tirado Herrero 2018).

Regarding access to housing, community land trusts (CLTs) have emerged as a way of ensuring long-term housing affordability via an arrangement where the Trust buys land and engages with prospective residents in a participatory process to co-create a housing scheme. The prospective homeowners thus hold a long-term renewable lease and profits from a potential sale are distributed between the previous owners and the Trust. In Washington DC, for example, in response to threats to affordable housing because of new developments, the Douglas Community Land Trust was created by residents and community representatives to "return power and decision-making in the hands of the community . . . via resident-controlled housing on community-owned land". Critiques of such solutions point out that the process of forming a land trust and providing access to housing is a slow process and presents challenges when it comes to scaling it up. However, CLTs are also formed toward objectives other than housing, such as to claim access to land, and reappropriate its uses and meanings toward emancipatory and decolonial horizons. Sogorea Te' Land Trust, for example, is an urban indigenous women-led land trust based in the San Francisco Bay Area and established in 2017 that facilitates the return of indigenous land to indigenous people.[2] Among many of its projects, the Trust has created an emergency response hub, in the face of climate and health crises, which includes a ceremonial space, food and medicine gardens, water catchment, filtration and storage, first-aid supplies, tools and a seed library.

New greening meets segregation and underinvestment in Anacostia, Washington DC

East of the Anacostia River in Washington DC encompasses areas such as Far Southeast/Southwest and Historic Anacostia, where the district's largest concentration of African American residents reside. According to the DC Fiscal Policy Institute, 92% of all residents living east of the river are Black, which reflects the legacy of segregation in the district and historic planning decisions, such as the construction of the 444-unit public housing complex Barry Farm demolished in 2019. Poverty rates east of the river also reached 33%, with almost 46% of all children living in poverty. It is also an area where only 20% of residents own their homes and as a result are particularly exposed to rent increases and displacement in the broader context of a city known as the most gentrified city in the United States, through both aggressive housing and commercial development.

In 2014, the fate of underinvested Anacostia started to change when OMA, a global New York City architecture firm, proposed a winning design for the 11th Street Bridge Park, a $50–60M development to enhance environmental and recreational access between both sides of the river while further cleaning up and revitalizing the two shorelines. The design brought much excitement to city planners and designers who quickly saw the opportunity to rebrand Anacostia as a place ripe for (green) redevelopment while leaving environmentally toxic sites such as the former waste incinerator at Kenilworth Park in Ward 7 and the lead toxicity around Barry Farms housing untreated. This choice showed the preference for enacting easily commodified emblematic projects rather than addressing existing environmental health hazards.

The bridge, planned for completion in 2024 (to date unbuilt), is underpinned by large non-profit efforts to include a comprehensive 2018 Equitable Development Plan, through which to implement intentional green, inclusive, healthy and affordable infrastructure (BBAR 2018). Among others, it includes a CLT, local workforce training and business development, and affirmative, anti-racism, cultural and green offerings. However, it is also deeply embedded in the local and city-wide history of unequal urban development. Barry Farm, the former public housing complex, will be redeveloped into a mixed-use, mixed-income, transit-oriented, open-space, new public infrastructure and recreation center which makes little room for the return of those previously displaced. Adjacent to Barry Farm is also the new development of Poplar Point, a mixed-use redevelopment including a new 70-acre park, solar panels, bike lanes and other transit-oriented features. However, only 10% of the 700–800 new units are reserved for affordable housing. Anacostia also hosts the Reunion Square development project, funded through a $60.8 million Tax Increment Financing tax scheme used to fund redevelopment projects in "emerging" neighborhoods, but which can trigger gentrification due to the nature of the new high-end housing.

Overall, critics tout the Bridge Park as a "bridge to gentrification", fearing that it will only attract physical and financial "gateway" projects to Anacostia oriented toward higher-class and white residents while commodifying concepts of greenness, culture and diversity through "cool" green and social venues. Although those venues are meant to serve the neighborhood, they will in effect rebrand it for the needs and uses of newcomers. Prices have been already increasing, and gentrification is looming in Anacostia, with median home prices having increased by 14.5% in August 2020 compared to the same month in 2019 (UrbanTurf 2020).

Eventually, no matter how much equity planning is embedded into greening interventions such as the Bridge Park, high-value "green" real estate projects might be directly paving the way for a new dispossession and displacement frontier. Such fears are justified, with some developers describing their vision to make the east of the river a "destination for residents from across the city" and a place where the firm "can own [the most] in the neighborhood". Unless more aggressive housing rights policies and related development taxes are put in place, Anacostia will likely become a white- and greenwashed gentrified neighborhood even before the Bridge Park project is completed.

Notes

1 This has been observed both at national level, as researched in Europe (Lancee and Van de Werfhorst 2012), and at the level of local urban communities, as shown in the case of the United States (van Holm 2019).
2 https://sogoreate-landtrust.org

Figure 2 Racialized or Ethnically Exclusionary Urbanization

2 Driver 2

Racialized or ethnically exclusionary urbanization

Race and ethnicity are foundational concepts when considering the justice implications of urban sustainability (Figure 2). We understand race as a term that "signifies and symbolizes sociopolitical conflicts and interests in reference to different types of human bodies" (Hesse 2007, 645, citing Winant 2001, 317). Race is not a biological category, but rather a socially and politically constructed marker of exclusion and discrimination, something worth noting due to long-standing and persistent positions stating the opposite (see Morning 2014). Ethnicity refers to a social group that shares a common and distinctive culture, religion and language. Racialized or ethnically exclusionary urbanization thus refers to urban development processes and outcomes that either unintentionally or purposefully ignore, dismiss or discount the experiences and realities of non-white and/or non-European origin residents. It also denotes the unequal impacts of urbanization on the lives, land, resources and practices of those groups, including sociospatial segregation, land grabbing, gentrification and displacement, or direct exclusion from the benefits of urban sustainability interventions, including green space, local food markets, renewable energy schemes or energy retrofitting, among others. The consequences of this historical and lasting process have become a hot-button issue in the United States in recent years. For example, in public and green spaces, the continued death of Black people at the hands of white police has raised profound questions about how changes in urban racial compositions precipitate changes in the policing and valuing of Black and brown bodies (Moore 2014) and produce controlling, surveillance and carceral practices (Pellow 2016).

As social constructs, race and ethnicity have very concrete impacts on our societal structures, the shaping of our urban environments and people's daily lives. There are, unfortunately, countless examples that show what happens in terms of urban sustainability and justice outcomes when racialized realities are not taken into account. One illustration is Detroit's

DOI: 10.4324/9781003221425-3

famed Eight Mile Road, which divides the majority, low-income African American city from its northern majority, upper-middle-income white suburb. Eight Mile is a racialized and classed border that sharply marks housing segregation patterns, access to educational opportunities and public and private transportation options (Mitchell 2018; Zernike 2016). In terms of transportation, Detroit's reputation as the Motor City meant that its highways were prioritized over mass transport systems, a factor that continues to shape the poor accessibility and under-maintenance of city bus services predominantly used by low-income Black female residents (Stovall 2019). On the other hand, recognizing and supporting different racialized experiences in urban spaces can create more inclusive sustainable interventions. Superkilen is an award-winning public space in Copenhagen's Nørrebro neighborhood that was created with residents from over 60 nationalities through an engaged and participatory planning process, developing a range of play, leisure and green infrastructures that meet the needs of different groups. Three distinct urban spaces for play, lingering and leisure were constructed over a half-a-mile linear tract of land, containing over 100 meaningful objects representing the different nationalities of neighborhood residents (Daly 2020).

Racial and ethnic segregation

Ghettos. Projects. These are just two words that represent urban spaces where racialized people, ethnic minorities and low-income people have historically been forced to dwell together in disinvested and neglected places that hold deep territorial stigmatization (Wacquant 2014). The word *ghetto* can be traced back to Italian cities in the sixteenth and seventeenth centuries when it was used to depict the quarters of segregated Jews. While segregation has always existed as an urban phenomenon, it was only in the 1920s, in the United States, that it began to be theorized as such, and its profound impacts were slowly understood. A century later, talking about "ghettos" still produces strong emotional, political and social responses.

Today, it is recognized that racial and ethnic segregation patterns have extremely deep roots. In the North American context, segregation's origin story begins with the forced removal and relocation of Native Americans through the 1830 Indian Removal Act to make room for white settlers and is later consolidated by the 1887 Dawes Act that converted communally held tribal lands into lots, two-thirds of which were given to white Americans (Solomon, Maxwell, and Castro 2019). Settler colonialism thus spatially differentiated and separated groups of people, with white people benefiting from new secure resources as Native Americans were dispossessed of their lands and livelihoods. In the American urban context, *redlining* became a foundational driver of segregation and increased socioeconomic inequality.

Redlining refers to mortgage loan risk assessment discrimination rules put in place by the Home Owners Loan Corporation and the Federal Housing Administration in the 1930s to decide what areas had access to low-cost mortgage lending as well as in many cases home insurance guaranteed by the government (Squires and Woodruff 2019).

Redlining ranked neighborhoods in descending order, from A to D, with A assigned to newer, affluent suburbs located away from city problems and D to non-white, generally urban neighborhoods (Pulido 2000). The latter became severely disinvested, reinforcing spatial segregation across US cities. They were so-called blighted neighborhoods with substantial white flight and urban renewal projects which demolished entire blocks of low-housing development (Vale 2013). Southwest in Washington DC, West End in Boston, SoMA and The Western Addition in San Francisco or the Gateway District in Minneapolis are just a few examples. The "clearing" of neighborhoods for urban renewal further isolated, scarred and divided them through the construction of highways and other road infrastructures, such as the I10 in New Orleans or Interstate 75–85 (the Downtown Connector) in Atlanta, through the 1956 Federal-Aid Highway Act. Sixty years later, 74% of D-ranked neighborhoods are low- to moderate-income, and nearly 63% are predominantly non-white (Mitchell and Franco 2018). This process of racial segregation sets the stage for persistent disparities between racialized and ethnic-minority groups in terms of access to parks, hospitals, street-lights and well-maintained roads (Solomon, Maxwell, and Castro 2019). Furthermore, many neighborhoods redlined in the 1930s, and subsequently suffering disinvestment for decades, began experiencing gentrification in the 1980s and 1990s (Wyly and Hammel 1999), including Jamaica Plain in Boston or U Street in Washington, leading to an influx of wealthier and whiter residents that displaced racialized minority groups.

The non-American experience of racial and ethnic segregation is more complex. A large body of work considering how segregation occurs in European cities has found a diversity of patterns of ethnic urban segregation, due to different welfare systems, migration patterns and political processes. As Sonia Arbaci (2019) underlines, urban and residential segregation is context-dependent, multiscalar and multifactor, with no "one-size-fits-all" model. Yet the shift in European approaches to address segregation—from more socialist-style, people-based infrastructure such as Les Grands Ensembles in cities like Paris, Lyon or Marseille in France, to neoliberal-inspired policies focusing on individuals and problematizing poor neighborhoods such as Glasgow's Transformation Regeneration Areas—has moved toward adopting North American ideas of ghettoization, with band-aid solutions rather than systemic ones. In Europe, area-based programs that address segregation and improve urban sustainability often do so through a discourse of urban regeneration, mixed communities or social mixing. The idea behind this strategy is to create a more socially mixed population (where mix refers to race, ethnicity and/or class) by adding more expensive housing to low-income areas either through wholesale redevelopment or by removing inexpensive dwellings through selected demolition and selling and upgrading existing housing. This process has been dubbed "gentrification by stealth" (Bridge, Butler, and Lees 2011) because gentrification has been found to lead to social segregation, social polarization and displacement.

The shift from people-based policies toward urban revitalization, as well as its impact, is well exemplified by Barcelona. In the first democratic elections after nearly 40 years of dictatorship under Franco, Barcelona's City Council devised new urban plans to provide much-needed social infrastructure to neighborhoods that sought "the creation of a balanced and integrated Barcelona, without segregation, with social and territorial equality for all citizens" (Calavita and Ferrer 2004, 60, citing Casas 1995). Shortly after, however, the city won the bid for the 1992 Olympic games. While at first this was seen as an opportunity to modernize Barcelona's infrastructure while retaining redistributive goals (McNeill 1999), urban interventions instead shifted almost entirely toward the mega-event demands of the Olympics, diminishing the social component present in the initial creation of public spaces and social infrastructures during the early 1980s (Anguelovski 2014). Thus the people-centered focus on the provision of infrastructure, especially to more marginalized populations, shifted toward a more tourist-driven, business-friendly urban development model, which triggered the gentrification of Ciutat Vella and Poblenou, among other areas. Despite this, Barcelona is still far from illustrating deep urban segregation. In extreme cases of racial and ethnic segregation, such as in South Africa, research has found that white residential areas have six-fold higher income, 12% greater tree cover, 9% higher vegetation greenness and are situated 700 m closer to public parks than areas with predominantly Black African, Indian and colored residents (Venter et al. 2020).

White privilege

Women's Studies scholar Peggy McIntosh brought the term white privilege in 1989 into everyday discourse with her popular essay titled

White Privilege: Unpacking the Invisible Knapsack. McIntosh writes from her experience of privilege based on having white skin color and being conditioned to be unaware of its existence, enumerating over two dozen everyday situations where being white has given her distinct advantages. White privilege exists because of historic processes of colonization and structural racism, the latter term pointing to how racism and white supremacy have become embedded in institutional, cultural and social practices and perpetuates inequities. For example, in settler colonial countries like Canada, Australia and the United States, the legal ability to claim property rights was contingent upon race, that is, being white. White privilege can be both unconsciously enjoyed *and* consciously perpetuated (Collins 2018). Ultimately, the term depicts a broader social system that operates to the benefit of whites and preserves their privilege—at the expense of non-whites (Pulido 2000). The concept, therefore, sits at the core of why racially and ethnically exclusive urbanization exists.

What does white privilege mean for the creation of injustices in the context of urban sustainability? First, a large and long-standing body of environmental justice research has shown how due to a range of policies, practices and social systems, environmental hazards have and continue to disproportionately impact low-income, especially non-white populations. This is called environmental racism. Scholar-activist Laura Pulido was among the first to show the importance of understanding environmental racism by looking at larger historical processes of urban development that have privileged white people (Pulido 2000). For example, the first suburbanization processes in Los Angeles at the start of the twentieth century arose in part because white middle-class people refused to live near immigrants and people of color. In this light, the residential desires and real estate interests of white residents were two important forces shaping the very development of the city (Ibid.). Similarly, a range of urban planning tools has also served to perpetuate white privilege, such as redlining, as discussed in the previous section. Another example is exclusionary zoning, a set of land use regulations that have long been used to keep people of lower economic brackets—and, though not specifically stated, of different races—out of certain neighborhoods. In June 2021, the US White House officially recognized how exclusionary zoning had created racial discrimination in the housing market (Rouse et al. 2021). Understanding the roots and perpetuation of environmental racism also requires unpacking how white privilege has shaped who is included and excluded from both environmental hazards and benefits.

Regarding environmental benefits, urban greening is a common and extensively used sustainability initiative explicitly connected with racialization. Urban growth, greening and whiteness have been found to be inextricably associated qualities of American cities (Connolly and Anguelovski 2021). This privilege was also illustrated through limited or whites-only access to urban nature and public spaces, including parks, boardwalks or swimming pools (Finney 2014). But this reality is not exclusive to American cities. Amsterdam Noord, long peripheral to the city despite its central location, is a historically Dutch white working-class neighborhood that has been rapidly changing since the 1960s due to a large influx of immigrants, mostly from Turkey and Morocco. The city of Amsterdam's New Urban Renewal strategy in the late 1990s underlined the spatial concentration of unemployment and ethnic minorities as a problem, their solution to which involved attracting more affluent, and whiter, residents through large investments in public space improvement and housing and infrastructure renovation (Pérez del Pulgar 2021). The Amsterdam example echoes area-based programs addressing segregation and illustrates how greening and urban sustainability processes are entangled in the process. It also echoes Sara Safransky's research (2014) in Detroit, where she has shown how the greening of postindustrial urban spaces, carried out under a market-based planning logic, operates to erase non-white cultural practices, in essence, a form of settler colonialism that creates and seizes a new frontier. Urban greening can thus become a sociospatial practice of white supremacy, exclusion and coercion of non-white practices in green spaces (Anguelovski and Connolly 2021). White privilege and what Park and Pellow (2011) call *environmental privilege*—the disproportionate access and benefit harnessed by white, upper-class residents vis-à-vis green and open spaces, waterfronts, fresh food, high-quality housing and recreational facilities—are therefore two sides of the same coin.

A final component of white privilege that deserves mention relates to how ideas of nature and green are translated into urban space. Hilary Angelo (2021) illustrates how urban nature came to be and is predominantly viewed as morally and universally good for all. Yet ideas of pristine nature and wilderness are mostly built on privileged white ideas of what nature is and should be, ignoring, for example, the legacy of oppression and violence against African American people in forests and other green spaces (Finney 2014). Beyond the United States, the idea of a manicured and formal nature for higher-income visitors and residents that exemplifies racialized exclusion from new green infrastructure can be seen in urban upgrading schemes in Rio de Janeiro (Comelli, Anguelovski, and Chu 2018) or in risk prevention and climate-adaptive green infrastructure in Medellin (Anguelovski, Irazábal-Zurita, and Connolly 2019b).

Grassroots action and policy tools

Some policy approaches have been adopted to redress racially and ethnically exclusive urbanization histories and patterns. One example is those policies that recognize the right of original residents to stay or return, designed to ensure that people with long-term connections to neighborhoods undergoing redevelopment or regeneration (see Chapter 3) are able to access affordable housing to stay or return there.

In Portland, Oregon, a right-to-return policy was used to counteract the city's long history of racial discrimination in housing and gentrification through the N/NE Neighborhood Housing Strategy (City of Portland n.d.). Albina, Portland's northeastern neighborhood, concentrated most of the city's Black population due to redlining practices. While it flourished economically despite a deteriorating housing stock and racist employment and financial practices, the community faced continuous disinvestment from the 1960s onward. Massive redevelopment projects displaced thousands of Black residents without replacement housing, despite city promises. Decades later, when a nearby development proposed in 2013 would disrupt another historic Black neighborhood, community leaders fought for the city to ensure that their residents would not be displaced. In 2015, the Portland Housing Bureau developed the N/NE Neighborhood Housing Strategy with $20 million in urban renewal funds to support affordable housing in the area, which includes loan assistance for home repair, down payment assistance for first-time homebuyers and the creation of new affordable housing. Priority is given to households whose homes were claimed by the city through eminent domain or who have received points based on a system that identifies a former or current address within areas identified to have been impacted by the city's racially discriminatory decisions (City of Portland n.d.). In practice, not all Albina residents have been able to benefit from the right-to-return policy due to their inability to purchase a home at current prices or the lack of official documentation to prove ownership.

Grassroots efforts to counteract racialized or ethnically exclusionary urbanization are burgeoning in the United States through revindications by Black Lives Matter, which seeks to think through and redress the socioeconomic and class underpinnings of anti-Blackness, white racial supremacy and policing (Moore 2014). Similarly, abolitionist movements directly address racist policing and city-making practices in their struggles to eradicate systematic and institutionalized oppression and violence, toward abolishing inequality. There is also emerging scholar-activist thinking about abolition ecologies and making "freedom as place", pushing for the need to examine urban natures first and foremost through the lens of anti-racist, postcolonial and indigenous theory (Heynen and Ybarra 2021; Simpson and Bagelman 2018).

Addressing compounded environmental racism in West Dallas

The community of West Dallas, now a collection of small neighborhoods still largely racially segregated, was established in 1886 but only formally incorporated into the city of Dallas in 1954. West Dallas has a long history of industrial concentration—including a lead plant, several concrete plants and other sites—with these industries long serving as an important source of employment for residents. One of the most notorious sites, Murphy Metals (later renamed RSR Corporation), opened in 1934 as a secondary lead smelter processing company (Cole 2021). Since that time, toxic land uses have accumulated throughout the neighborhoods of West Dallas and along its bordering Trinity River. Racial segregation is a complex story in West Dallas because the area has always been occupied by a mix of Latinx, Black and white residents. These dimensions of race, ethnicity and class have combined to shape uneven access to urban infrastructure, basic services and sustainability projects, as West Dallas was historically deprived of park space, transit and even road infrastructure—with some areas lacking paved roads until the 1980s (Wiltz 2018). Until 2013, West Dallas remained separated from the rest of the city by the Trinity River and the I-30 highway until the opening of the Margaret Hunt Hill Bridge and still lacks basic environmental facilities such as fresh and affordable grocery stores.

While at least parts of West Dallas were segregated even in the 1880s, in the 1940s urban planner Harland Bartholomew formally designated and cut off "Negro-districts" from the rest of the city while preventing Black families from buying homes outside those limits. After World War II (WWII) and postwar job contraction, many white families and some wealthier Blacks left West Dallas for areas with better jobs north of the river. By the time of Dallas's school desegregation in the 1970s, which was extremely late in the US context where most schools were desegregated during the 1960s, 85% of the residents identified as Blacks (Cole 2021). This segregation endures today with a clear color-coded division of Dallas neighborhoods between the west and east as Latinx, south and some west as Black and white in the North. As of the late 2010s, West Dallas is 70% Hispanic although some small areas such as Muncie and Westmoreland Heights remain mainly Black (Ibid. 2021). Consequently, according to a 2018 report by the Urban Institute, Dallas is still the least inclusive city in the country, with overlapping racial segregation and economic exclusion (Poethig et al. 2018).

In line with other environmental justice struggles in the rest of the United States, West Dallas residents mobilized against environmental toxics in the 1980s and obtained the closure of the RSR smelting plant in 1984 and its subsequent Superfund site designation in 1995, which was followed by some clean-up efforts. Although this period also opened up opportunities for neighborhood revitalization efforts, echoing trends across the United States, Dallas extensively demolished public housing and many private homes, displacing mostly African American families. Revitalization efforts also translated into many unfulfilled city-driven revitalization visions around the river and adjacent contaminated or abandoned sites.

Yet, during the late 2000s and 2010s, some areas of West Dallas became host to emblematic infrastructure that prompted new commercial, residential and leisure investment and its use by mostly white, upper-class residents. In 2012, the Margaret Hunt Hill Bridge became a symbol for a new, revitalized and "connected" West Dallas, while environmental toxics continue unabated in the racialized areas of the neighborhood. In 2016, the Argos concrete plant was relocated from what is now the site of the Trinity Groves luxury development to the vicinity of a public school that was subsequently closed due to underperformance (Cole 2021). Together with the bridge, new green amenities are planned and financed in West Dallas, including the $60M Harold Simmons Park. Long-term residents are perceiving such infrastructure as tools to spark investment and demographic change rather than as amenities for long-term residents. In contrast to these iconic infrastructure improvements, which further root white privilege in Dallas, Latinx and Black residents are asking for small-scale improvements, including new amenities in existing parks and a recognition of their long-term use and relationship with the Trinity River.

Despite new manifestations of injustices, however, the city is not leaving the legacy of racial segregation and white privilege fully unattended. In the past few years, Dallas has committed to funding the rehabilitation of long-term residents' homes, supporting their home-buying abilities and home improvement efforts through low-interest loans, and offering taxes and funding mechanisms to developers (such as a waiver to building and development fees) investing in changing neighborhoods like West Dallas. While these measures aim to prevent further displacement, the broader policy context in the State of Texas undermines social equity and affordable housing efforts by banning tools like linkage fees for new home construction and inclusionary zoning. That West Dallas is gentrifying does not prevent its Latinx and Black communities from being threatened by new contaminating industries. In 2021, the renewal permit granted to the roofing company, GAF Materials Corporation, against which residents had been mobilizing, risks further perpetuating environmental inequities (Cole, Reyes Jr., and Bazan 2021).

Figure 3 Uneven Urban Intensification and Regeneration

3 Driver 3

Uneven urban intensification and regeneration

The concept of uneven development (Figure 3) has long been used in critical geography to denote how specific urban forms and their socioeconomic relations are shaped by cycles of capital accumulation and devaluation and the social processes that mediate them (Smith 2010; Harvey 2014). Uneven development is, in other words, the geographical manifestation of capitalist urban development. Uneven development, explored in depth in this chapter, is a useful frame to understand two critical, interconnected dynamics underway in many cities across the world today. On the one hand, there have been unprecedented rates of urbanization in recent decades, with urban areas expanding twice as fast as their populations (Angel et al. 2011). This staggering figure gives a sense of the magnitude of urban change: the built environment across the globe increased by 1,130 standard football fields ($7,140\,m^2$) *per day* from 2001 to 2018, with China accounting for almost half of new urbanization (Sun et al. 2020). On the other hand, there has been widespread redevelopment of existing urban areas—historic centers, underinvested suburbs or previously industrialized areas—through public or public/private financing schemes under a process called *urban regeneration* or *revitalization*. Due to what is often a blatant prioritization of economic goals of redevelopment over social or environmental goals, some authors argue that urban regeneration or revitalization are code words for the erasure of working-class districts and the attraction of wealthier residents, or in short, gentrification (Smith 1996). How urban growth and regeneration happen, and who decides and is able to participate in the process, are critical questions when considering the drivers of urban justice in the context of urban sustainability.

An increase in both urban intensification and urban regeneration can drive injustice when land, housing, public space or green space compete with one another and are reconfigured in ways that have negative impacts on vulnerable residents (Gould and Lewis 2016). Inequitable impacts and processes have been observed in a variety of urban sustainability interventions

DOI: 10.4324/9781003221425-4

including eco-districts, transit-oriented development, green building, greenways and other types of "resilient" infrastructures (see Chapter 5). Urban intensification and urban regeneration do not stand alone as drivers of injustice but are principally linked to material and livelihood inequalities (Chapter 1), neoliberal development and growth (Chapter 10), and the limitations of existing forms of civic participation (Chapter 8). In this chapter we explore in depth how processes of urban densification and expansion as well as urban regeneration or revitalization have unfolded across the world and their connection to sustainability and the drivers of urban injustice.

Urban growth: sprawl, densification and expansion

Over half the world's population lives in cities. Indeed, it is estimated that nearly two-thirds of the world's population will be urban by 2030, with urban growth extending and generating deeper climate change impacts, income inequalities and environmental degradation. According to UN Habitat's World Cities Report 2020, 96% of urban growth in the coming decade will occur in the less developed regions of East Asia, South Asia and Africa, with India, China and Nigeria accounting for 35% of the total increase in global urban population from 2018 to 2050.

While urban sprawl—characterized by scattered, low-density, leapfrog and single-use development with often poor transit connections to the urban core—is the predominant term used to describe urbanization and suburbanization in the United States (Ewing 1997), in the Global South, urban expansion is more frequently used to describe city growth that lacks typical US-style characteristics (Li, Wei, and Korinek 2018). Social and behavioral researchers underline personal choice and racial relations as key factors behind urban sprawl, while institutional approaches to urban sprawl and urban expansion consider the exceptional role of local government (Wei and Ewing 2018). Be it sprawl or expansion, due to dynamics of uneven development, both are connected to densification and have important socioenvironmental implications, ultimately driving old and new types of urban injustice.

Studies have found correlations between urban sprawl, income inequality and segregation (Jargowsky 2002), and scholars agree that urban sprawl has increased racial and gender inequality due to how it shapes access to urban services and employment (McLafferty and Preston 1992). In the United States, white flight to newly expanded suburbs during the 1960s and 1970s devalued the land and home prices in inner-city districts, which ended up mostly inhabited by racialized minorities, while creating new infrastructure and services for white residents moving to the suburbs (McClintock 2011). This process created what McClintock calls "demarcated devaluation" for places such as West Oakland (Ibid.), Boston's Roxbury neighborhood (Anguelovski 2014) or West Dallas (Cole 2021), among many others. Negative human and environmental health is also associated with urban sprawl, due to increased traffic congestion and thus poorer air quality, reduced physical activity and increased obesity, among others (Ewing et al. 2003). At the same time, because urban sprawl during the 1980s and 1990s was often connected to the densification of urban centers for business and entertainment, the availability, size and maintenance of public green space for residents who remained in the city core were significantly reduced (Anguelovski 2014; Boone et al. 2009). In Baltimore, for example, Black residents have historically had access to smaller, under-maintained and under-upgraded parks in comparison with white residents who had moved away from the urban core (Boone et al. 2009).

In more recent decades, while increasing urban densification has been credited with reducing sprawl through "smart growth" approaches in the United States, it is also linked to the gentrification of previously "undesirable" areas. For example, Austin, known as the greenest city in Texas, has opted for densification as a solution to the challenge of balancing growth, equity and environmental quality (Connolly and Lira 2021). Yet the decision to preserve abundant green spaces in West Austin and implement a smart growth plan to densify East Austin has been used by public officials and private developers as a tool to attract investment and a form of green city branding, resulting in densification that has directly displaced Black and Latino residents (Ibid.). Segregation and white privilege, explained in Chapter 2, are deeper historical processes that have driven this combination of urban sprawl and densification.

Studies projecting urban expansion in Global South cities over the coming decades underscore a significant loss of habitat in biodiversity hotspots and the reduction of tropical carbon biomass (Seto, Güneralp, and Hutyra 2012). A large body of literature exists on China's urban expansion due to its rapid urban transformation in recent decades, with unprecedented rates of land development and changes in urban form that have exacerbated a range of inequalities (mobility, access to housing, etc.) that began to emerge in previous decades due to capitalist-oriented economic reforms and urban spatial restructuring (Schneider, Chang, and Paulsen 2015). Nanjing, part of one of the largest emerging global city regions in the world along the Yangtze River Delta, illustrates a typical scenario of how land development and urban expansion in China are used by local government to drive economic growth, despite the uneven and inequitable outcomes it produces (Wei 2015). This urban sprawl drives land grabs, leads to the destruction of productive formal and informal farming land and forces the mass migration of farmers to newly built urban centers, thereby losing both their livelihoods and networks (Wang, Shi, and Zhou 2020).

Finally, urban densification, in contexts of sprawl or expansion, can limit the options for more sustainable or nature-based infrastructure, and this increases the environmental impact of cities through waste production, water management and overall pollution. Densely populated housing estates, for example, limit the possibility of making major changes to the surrounding physical environment. This "space scarcity" must be understood through the lens of inequality, as it is often the poorest residents who inhabit those overly dense neighborhoods with crowded homes in poor physical conditions, and gray-dominated or limited public spaces. Densification goals and their associated efficiency and sustainability claims can also undermine local social benefits and bottom-up sustainability initiatives such as community gardens that have to compete with real estate speculation and tourist-oriented developments. In Barcelona, for example, the Hort de la Vanguardia community garden was removed in 2021 to make space for the front entrance of a major new hotel in the neighborhood of Poblenou (Kotsila, Anguelovski et al. 2021).

Urban regeneration as gentrification?

Urban regeneration, revitalization, renewal, renaissance: for several decades now urban policy across the world has focused on putting these concepts into practice. While urban regeneration, urban renewal or urban redevelopment are the most used terms, all of them refer to public or public/private investment in spaces or neighborhoods that have been marginalized or become derelict after a period of economic and social neglect. Urban regeneration/revitalization is thus about the management and planning of existing urban areas, rather than planning and developing new urbanization (Couch and Fraser 2003).

A vast and varied literature exists on urban regeneration and urban revitalization, growing out of the decades-old UK and US urban policy agendas that have spread globally. Contributions that approach the topic from a policymaking perspective generally point to best practices and consider regeneration/revitalization in a positive light and as a technical question of governance (Couch, Fraser, and Percy 2003). Physical interventions often play a key role in regeneration/revitalization strategies such as business improvement districts, flagship developments or events that catalyze surrounding urban change (Hoyt 2006). City marketing and rebranding also plays a fundamental role in attracting tourism, real estate development and other industries to invest and partake in the "new" city. In this light, Richard Florida's (2002) canonical and controversial work *The Rise of the Creative Class* has had an enormous impact on regeneration strategies globally. Florida argues that creative individuals and industries, attracted by "authenticity" and "quality of place" can advance urban economic success. This is well illustrated by the sustainable regeneration strategies unfolding in North Glasgow's Forth and Clyde Canal area, where "cultural regeneration" has been the driver. Lower land values were leveraged to encourage the relocation of national organizations like the Scottish Opera, the National Theatre of Scotland and the establishment of an arts-based community interest company, while Scottish Canals attracted the creative class by converting the Whiskey Bond building into creative industry co-working spaces. While this arts-based regeneration approach has been proclaimed a success by public and private sectors in Glasgow, a new community of art professionals is largely disconnected from the history of the area and its long-term residents (Garcia-Lamarca and Gray 2020). This underlines how urban regeneration may radically alter areas toward a new vision and attractiveness defined by and for non-residents.

Sustainability has become a core part of urban regeneration or revitalization policy and planning discourse since the late 1990s, though not so much in project implementation (Lombardi et al. 2011; Korkmaz and Balaban 2020). The idea behind bringing together urban regeneration and sustainability is to improve the environmental quality of historically neglected neighborhoods while addressing so-called social ills. Often, these are neighborhoods in dense historic centers with degraded housing stock, poor street and service infrastructure, and low quality and availability of public green space. Cases of large-scale "sustainable" historic center regeneration include the Old Town (Ciutat Vella) in Barcelona, Seun in Seoul and Chinatown in Boston. Other policies have focused on postindustrial neighborhoods, combining land clean-up and regeneration with access to a new large green and blue space, or housing stock conversion and construction, such as in Saint-Henri, Montreal, Canada, or the Liverpool Waterfront in the UK. Finally, municipal and metropolitan agencies, especially in Europe, have reinvested resources in stigmatized suburban areas like *Les Grands Ensembles* in French cities such as Saint Denis or Issy-Les-Moulineaux and expanded the housing stock (often through demolition), public space and sustainable transport linkages. Though the premise of urban regeneration and improved livability is to lift residents of "sensitive urban zones" (in French, *zones urbaines sensibles*) out of social exclusion, marginalization, deprivation and insecurity (Couch, Sykes, and Börstinghaus 2011), few are the examples that have achieved these objectives in practice.

Due to the depoliticized nature of urban regeneration/revitalization, many critical urban scholars argue that these terms are code words for gentrification, maintaining that regeneration is fundamentally about the influx of a middle-upper income population that displaces long-term working-class residents (Smith 1996). Especially in historic urban centers, neighborhood revitalization or regeneration is often exclusionary, having been implemented without taking into account the vulnerability or needs of long-term residents in the context of free-market rentals and real estate. Despite the supposed sustainability dimensions of urban revitalization, whereby economic, social and environmental interventions are integrated to create denser, more efficient cities with supposedly "trickle-down" benefits (Anguelovski 2014), these interventions can drive inequality when they are centrally planned and ignore the needs and demands of long-term residents. This is exemplified by Turkey's North Ankara Urban Regeneration Project (NAURP), the largest so-called "sustainable" urban regeneration project in the country. The NAURP was formulated in response to decades of illegal development and squatter settlements that sprouted south of Ankara's airport, seeking to reverse the urban decline and create a healthier urban environment (Korkmaz and Balaban 2020). Despite implementing one of the largest green areas in Ankara, the NAURP neglected the social and economic dimensions fundamental to sustainable regeneration: residents had no voice in the process and were merely "informed" of it; rent aids provided during the regeneration process were insufficient; and employment opportunities were not created for local residents, to name a few problems (Ibid.).

Finally, scholars have recently highlighted the colonial and racialized dimensions of urban regeneration by illustrating how renewed public or public/private investment in previously neglected areas is linked to the erasure and dispossession of non-white populations. Grandinetti (2019) outlines how redevelopment plans for the Kaka'ako renewal district in Honolulu, Hawai'i, transformed the urban landscape to produce more surplus value and changed the urban social fabric by making white settlers and upper-class Japanese the protagonists of this new redeveloped Kaka'ako, while suppressing the Native Hawaiian community. Regeneration is also a code word for increased surveillance and control of non-white bodies and practices, as a result of new preferences, norms and accepted behavior imposed by white residents (Wiig 2018; Samara 2010). In their activist mapping work analyzing the redevelopment of the Russell neighborhood in West Louisville, Kentucky, Root Cause Research Center found that changes in nuisance laws and increased police surveillance directly correlate to the increased criminalization of Black residents (Root Cause Research Center 2021). This process occurred in parallel with land transfers for market-rate development actively backed and supported by the local government. Activists argue that the intensified policing that became part of the Russel gentrification process led to the murder of 26-year-old Emergency Room technician and Black Louisville resident Breonna Taylor in her home by the Louisville Metro Police Department, continuing the city's legacy of plantation urbanism (Poe and Bellamy 2020). Especially in the American context, nuisance law operates through sociospatial histories of racial capitalism and reorganizes property relations to set the stage for the redevelopment of "nuisance" neighborhoods (Graziani et al. 2022). Some further link this increased control with the deployment of smart city narratives and technologies as a form of "military urbanism" (Wiig 2018). These cases underline how "sustainable" urban regeneration/revitalization can become intertwined with property ownership, urban speculation, race and policing, exacerbating existing socioeconomic inequality.

Grassroots action and policy tools

Some policy and planning tools do exist to address uneven urban intensification and regeneration. Speculative development that often accompanies both processes can be controlled to some degree through policies including strict regulations on touristic and short-term rental housing or vacant property like in Vancouver, Canada, moratoriums on new hotels or hospitality industry permits like in Barcelona, Spain or rent controls or decreases like in Berlin, Germany, in order to provide a buffer for local residents to avoid being priced out of the neighborhood or displaced by urban transformations (BCNUEJ 2021). Adopting such tools and applying a genuinely grounded, justice-oriented approach to urban expansion, densification or regeneration requires city governments to prioritize social and environmental goals over economic ones. Due to the strong influence of the real estate, tourism and business-friendly industry sectors in general, and the dependence of many municipalities on increasing property values and taxes for their budgetary needs, this is unfortunately not a popular, nor even politically feasible stance in many cities.

The title of Porter and Shaw's (2013) excellent volume on urban expansion, densification and regeneration provides the key question when addressing urban justice: *Whose Urban Renaissance?* In seeking alternatives to gentrification cloaked as urban renaissance by neoliberal governments, the stories from various cities around the world show how urban regeneration can sometimes turn out in better-than-expected ways, thanks to local limits or organized struggles that fight for and win concessions from the state and the market. In terms of such struggles, Pascual-Molinas and Ribera-Fumaz (2013) provide a nuanced account of how grassroots opposition and resistance to city council regeneration plans can shape new policy designs that benefit the many rather than the few. For example, residents in Barcelona's Sant Pere and Santa Catarina neighborhoods came together in the early 2000s to fight for urban regeneration that met their needs, in response to a public space slated to become a parking lot which they dubbed the "hole of shame" (Anguelovski 2014). After years of conflict and ad hoc use of the space as a community garden, plaza, playground and sports field, in 2007 the city agreed to build a permanent multiuse green space and remained more receptive to the needs of local residents in subsequent regeneration projects in Ciutat Vella (Pascual-Molinas and Ribera-Fumaz 2013). But our knowledge of urban regeneration projects in Barcelona today suggests that these gains can be short-lived. In Santa Caterina, the growth of mass tourism fed by urban regeneration in and around the "hole of shame" project has compromised residential access to playgrounds, increased street crime, and a weakened sense of place and collective trust (Oscilowicz et al. 2020). Furthermore, as the technology, smart-city-driven regeneration of the Poblenou district shows, mobilization and continued struggle is fundamental in ensuring more just and inclusive urban environments for all (BCNUEJ 2022).

Greening the neoliberal pill in Hellenikon, Athens

Athens did not integrate conscientious urban planning into the rapid 1960s urbanization processes up until 1985. As a result, many of the city and surrounding municipalities developed abruptly and with little consideration for quality public space, ranking Athens as one of the worst cities for access to green space in Europe (0.97 m²/person in 2012 according to UN Habitat). Urban regeneration only made its official debut in 1983 in Athens' first Urban Master Plan. It is in this context that Hellenikon—the former site of Athens' airport briefly envisioned as one of Europe's largest public green spaces—was ultimately hijacked by elite economic interests in the spirit of neoliberal austerity politics implanted in Greece following the 2008 financial crisis. The resulting plan for the development of Hellenikon demonstrates urban regeneration processes that (re)produce inequalities in the distribution and accessibility of environmental and social goods.

When the airport moved from Hellenikon to East Attica, according to Law 233 of 1995: "the land of the ex-airport [was] to be mainly used for the creation of a metropolitan green zone". This newly available plot of land, near the city center and strategically positioned facing the Agios Kosmas coastal area, sparked much civic, political and economic interest and discussions around its future use. At the time, Athens was undergoing a series of changes in planning legislation and new infrastructure development as a result of its selection as the host city of the 2004 Olympic Games. In the months running up to the games, three years after the Hellenikon site became available, the Greek Ministry of

Environment launched an international competition for the creation of a metropolitan park in Hellenikon, envisioned primarily as a large public green space for recreation, with only 10% of the area dedicated to economic activities that would provide for its maintenance (Apostolopoulou and Kotsila 2021). Even this distribution was contested by the four adjunct municipalities denouncing the privatization and economic exploitation of the last vast, free and potentially green space in Athens.

Gradually, however, Hellenikon went from an inclusive park ambition to a speculation target for foreign capital investment. Faced by one of the most severe economic depressions in the post-2009 period, Greece received financial assistance from the EU and the International Monetary Fund and committed to the implementation of two Economic Adjustment Programs. In 2011, Hellenikon was deemed an asset for capitalization as part of the conditions set by international creditors for economic recovery, yet the space was highly contested. In the meantime, a strong grassroots movement that had emerged throughout the intense sociopolitical turmoil in Greece had claimed the abandoned space for social and solidarity activities (i.e., the Metropolitan Community Clinic in Hellenikon,[1] and one of the most emblematic cases of community urban agriculture, the Hellenikon community garden[2]), and fought for an alternative and socioecologically sustainable "Park for all in Hellenikon". Despite these efforts, the then left-wing government of SYRIZA succumbed to the creditors' demands.

The Investment Development Plan for Hellenikon was released and approved in the summer of 2017, leaving the overall process of selling out common wealth almost entirely outside of democratic control. According to the plan, the green space portion of the park would only take up one-third of the whole 620 ha area, and include 22 ha of culture, recreation and sports-related infrastructure. Most importantly, the park was to be situated in the middle of a wider urban development of villas and luxury apartments, a casino, 5-star luxury hotels, theme sights, entertainment venues and malls (IDP 2017), clearly aimed at upper-class consumers, residents and tourists. The placement of the park, surrounded by high-end infrastructure, with only a few access points from the city and with no direct connection to the coast, reflects the characteristics of a green luxury enclave rather than that of an open, accessible and welcoming green amenity destined for the wider public.

In 2019, the newly elected right-wing government announced the development of Hellenikon as one of its top priorities. As of 2022, the space is awaiting construction, set to provide the much-needed access to urban nature only to a privileged few and restrict its climate mitigation and adaptation functions (heat refuge, water drainage, CO_2 capture, sustainable economic activities and reuse of existing infrastructure) only to those who can afford to reside there or consume in its surroundings. Public disappointment about the fate of Hellenikon runs deep due to its non-participatory nature and its disregard for the concerns and proposals that social movements had put forward in previous years. Guided by political pressures hinged on the "there-is-no-alternative" neoliberal logic of privatization, Hellenikon compromises environmental justice in distributive, procedural and recognition aspects, even if materially it remains to be realized.

Notes

1 www.mkiellinikou.org/en/
2 http://agroselliniko.blogspot.com/

Figure 4 Unequal Environmental Health and Pollution Patterns

4 Driver 4

Unequal environmental health and pollution patterns

Environmental health traditionally refers to the branch of public health concerned with the link between human health and the environments people inhabit. As stated by the World Health Organization, there are multiple prerequisites for good health which depend on the status of proximate environments at various scales, such as "clean air, stable climate, adequate water, sanitation and hygiene, safe use of chemicals, protection from radiation, healthy and safe workplaces, sound agricultural practices, health-supportive cities and built environments, and a preserved nature". The interdependency of human and non-human systems becomes more and more foregrounded in science and society and is increasingly cast in terms of human health impacts in light of the COVID-19 pandemic. The radical interconnections between environmental, biological and sociocultural systems at global and local scales have become more evident than ever. This has strong implications for how we conceptualize and enact socioenvironmental justice. Environmental health factors encompass all aspects of life in our physical surroundings which can potentially increase or reduce the risk of disease, as well as broader factors of physical and mental illness or well-being. In the context of cities, access to things like public transportation and other utilities, supporting social networks and broader social capital, employment and other facilitating economic structures have been shown to shape mental and physical health outcomes (Duncan and Kawachi 2018). Limited access to or lack of these infrastructures is often a result of historical patterns of exclusion like structural racism that eventually led to poor health and health inequalities (Bailey et al. 2017).

Environmental injustice thus occurs when lower income, historically marginalized or racialized groups are disproportionately exposed to pollution, conditions of climate-related (health) risks or have unequal access to benefits of environmental amenities (Figure 4). Uneven environmental health patterns in cities can be both an expression and a driver of further

DOI: 10.4324/9781003221425-5

injustice. This can be understood, for example, through the concept of *syn-demics* in health (Fronteira et al. 2021) in the context of the COVID-19 pandemic, where multiple interrelated health injustices produce compound outcomes of ill health. Studies following the spread of COVID-19 in the Global North, for example, show that low-income and racialized residents have faced a greater risk of infection and death due to their living, working and environmental conditions (Cole et al. 2020). The same groups have historically faced higher rates of asthma (Williams, Sternthal, and Wright 2009), a disease linked to environmental air pollution and poor housing conditions (e.g., exposure to mold) that can exacerbate the severity of COVID-19 (Hegde 2020).

Urban environmental justice has emerged as a field of both scientific inquiry and civic contestation, strongly motivated by the need to address unequal health patterns in urban neighborhoods. Importantly, environmental justice is not only about fighting the unequal distribution of risk to the physical conditions that produce ill health but also about "rebuilding community and remaking place" (Anguelovski 2013), improving neighborhood environments while empowering local communities to enact sustainability, environmental revitalization and climate adaptation.

Unequal exposure to environmental contamination and toxicity

Environmental justice scholars have extensively documented how lower-income and racialized populations have historically suffered worse-quality living environments and higher exposure to pollutants. They emphasize how environmental health injustice and the unequal distribution of environmental risk are fundamentally underpinned by social relations and processes produced through the political economies of uneven development, investment and growth of different communities (Foster 1998; Shi et al. 2016). It is telling that in cities across the United States, Europe, China and elsewhere, increases in inequality in relation to income, education levels and access to housing are accompanied by worsening segregation patterns which were found to have direct and dire impacts on health and well-being (Cole et al. 2017; see also Chapter 1). In segregated neighborhoods, poverty, disinvestment and lack of access to political power intersect to create environmental injustices (Williams and Collins 2016).

In the Global North, and the United States in particular, entrenched segregation, zoning ordinances and lack of political power have led to the placement of hazardous waste and toxic facilities in the vicinity of poor and minority neighborhoods, as Dorceta Taylor and others have demonstrated

(Taylor 2014). Decisions on placement are underpinned by deeper historical and social mechanisms of racism, inequality and exclusion that make it impossible for affected communities to "just leave" such risky environments (Ibid.). Indeed, it is the racialization of a neighborhood that attracts noxious facilities, and not the other way around (Mohai and Saha 2015). Laura Pulido further explores how these processes of environmental racism against racialized and minority populations occur in the context of white privilege, racialized capitalism and state-sanctioned violence. This can be described as the state-facilitated socioeconomic ability of private businesses and corporations to capture and secure benefits for and alongside a white elite—in this case, that of living in clean, green, healthy (suburban) neighborhoods away from industrial contamination and non-white people (Pulido 2008).

These insights are crucial for how urban landscapes are understood and inform plans for sustainability globally. Namely, they remind us that land values, public space amenities and other markers of neighborhood livability are produced historically through the parallel processes of exclusion and privilege (see Chapters 2 and 3). Disadvantaged racialized or ethnically diverse (i.e., non-majority white) neighborhoods or districts tend to suffer most from pollution, as in the case of outdoor air toxics in southern California and associated cancer risks (Morello-Frosch, Pastor, and Sadd 2001), and more broadly in the case of exposure to noxious low-quality environments for Black, Latinx and people of color in the United States (Bryant and Mohai 2019).

Italy's southern region of Campania, one of the poorest and most densely populated regions in the country, also has a long history of environmental injustice dating back to the 1980s. The lack of proper waste management in the area has been accompanied by perpetuated illegal dumping of toxic garbage near inhabited areas; a practice that was tolerated by authorities and supported by local criminal organizations. While powerful para-legal elites have extracted rent over the territory that was used as a "dump" (De Rosa 2018), marginalized residents have suffered high rates of cancer, among other health problems, that have often been ignored or denied in mainstream political and scientific discourse. This example illustrates how uneven patterns of environmental health are not only an issue of justice in terms of distribution but also in terms of whose narratives are acknowledged as valid by institutions and can feed into the policy (see Chapter 9).

Environmental exclusions and their impact on health are also tied to procedural injustices and lack of meaningful participatory processes engaging historically marginalized groups. In Surat, India, for example, while the city government recognized the increasingly pressing need for climate adaptation infrastructure, especially for vulnerable groups, civil engagement has been shown to be ad hoc and focused on sectoral advisory groups, scientific experts and key stakeholders (Chu, Anguelovski, and Carmin 2015). As a result, the accrued benefits of interventions in public health, water supply and urban economic development were unclear in terms of improving the capacity of poor people to adapt to climate change, while specific adaptation projects indicated further distributional injustices for vulnerable groups (Ibid.).

The case of Chester, Pennsylvania, USA, is also emblematic of the historical struggles of the environmental justice movement. As a predominantly Black region with high poverty rates (31% in 2019), Chester is home to some of the most polluting facilities, including the nation's largest waste incinerator, a sewage sludge incinerator, a paper mill that burns coal waste and petroleum coke, numerous chemical plants and other toxic waste sites. As Foster (1998) argues for the case of Chester, "the combination of white flight and limited residential choices, likely due to a combination of poverty and housing discrimination, along with falling property values, left poor people of color essentially trapped in environmentally subordinate neighborhoods". At the same time, processes of consultation with government representatives in Chester were ridden with technical language and condescending notes, leading to grassroots protests and a long-term struggle against the environmental hazard these facilities were posing to the community. It became clear that the issue of justice, at its core, was about the agency, representation and participation of low-income African American communities in decision-making processes that would directly and fundamentally affect their lives (Ibid.).

As stated earlier, patterns of health inequality through the unequal distribution of environmental harms and benefits are not only a product of lower land values that facilitate polluting industries to locate their facilities in these areas but also because residents of these neighborhoods are less able to mobilize political power to advocate for improved environmental conditions on their behalf (Mohai and Saha 2015). Both aspects hide structural drivers and historical patterns of social exclusion and discrimination and are not simply the outcome of unjust decisions about the siting off toxic facilities. Although many grassroots efforts fighting exposure to environmental risk have been successful in articulating new modes of sustainability and of resisting further health risk exposures, it is such neighborhoods and their inhabitants that often become stigmatized, "ghetto-ised" and systematically excluded from conversations about urban sustainability and health taking place at the policymaking level. In the next section, we discuss how a new paradigm of making cities greener and climate resilient is often ridden with the same tensions between advancing ecological and economic sustainability while advancing social and environmental justice.

Unequal access to the sustainable, climate-proof and healthy city

Policies that enhance sustainable mobility, support energy-efficient housing or provide community-managed land for urban agriculture can provide benefits for ecological sustainability while also enhancing the health and well-being of urban residents. But when such initiatives are mostly destined for privileged neighborhoods, or accessible only to privileged groups, uneven and unjust patterns of health emerge. In Barcelona, for example, schools in richer neighborhoods have more green spaces, with important implications for the mental and behavioral health of poorer sociodemographics (Pérez-del-Pulgar et al. 2021). When it comes to sustainable energy infrastructure in rehabilitated or new housing, research has shown that the demographics already suffering energy poverty are the same as those with less access to renewable energy sources and energy-efficient features, thus remaining exposed to health risks related to the cold and wet environment such as mold-related asthma, or heat stress episodes during hot summer days (Grossmann et al. 2021). As extreme temperatures more frequently impact cities around the world (Romanello et al. 2021), energy poverty and the lack of appropriate infrastructure are increasing climate-related health vulnerability. Many poor households in Europe, for example, in the context of rising fuel prices and austerity policies, have resorted to burning unsuitable and unsafe materials to keep warm, leading to intense air pollution inside homes and around entire neighborhoods (Thomson, Snell, and Bouzarovski 2017). In contrast, it has also been observed that low-carbon interventions such as energy-efficient housing or public transit improvements, run the risk of laying the groundwork for gentrification and displacement (Blok 2020). In the district of Nordhavn in Copenhagen, for example, where most residents live in energy-efficient homes, home prices are much higher than average, contributing to what has been called "low-carbon gentrification" (Bouzarovski, Frankowski, and Tirado Herrero 2018).

It is clear then that urban injustice in terms of health can be driven by existing imbalances of power and privilege that translate into uneven abilities to adapt to socioenvironmental changes such as those created by climate change. In regions such as Central America and the Caribbean, for example, hazard-prone environments have co-evolved with histories of colonization, dispossession, social inequality and poverty, to produce unequal disasters and the commodification of disaster-related recovery, as was noted in Puerto Rico, after hurricane Maria in 2017 (Cruz-Martínez et al. 2018). The storm decimated the already deficient electricity network on the island, compromising several core services including healthcare, but the resilience of renewable energy initiatives proposed by local communities proved high.

However, the lack of public participation in the post-hurricane context, ignoring the work and success of such grassroots initiatives, perpetuated both socioenvironmental inequalities and the democratic dysfunctions of the past (Bui 2018). The privatization of electricity, and other top-down articulations of energy sustainability that followed, revealed deep concerns over the transparency of decision-making in energy governance, with direct impacts on health.

It is crucial also to note how processes of social marginalization and health inequalities in the "sacrifice zones" of urban peripheries, or in derelict and disinvested historical city centers, often occur in parallel to processes of gentrification elsewhere. In the case of Campania, Italy, discussed earlier, the gradual transformation of Naples' peri-urban areas into "social dumps" exposed to toxicity and associated health risks was accompanied by inner-city gentrification driven by tourism and urban elites (Armiero and D'Alisa 2012). Along these lines, Anguelovski et al. (2016) note that land use planning for climate adaptation can exacerbate sociospatial inequality through "acts of commission", by which poor communities are negatively affected or displaced, and as "acts of omission", by which elite groups are prioritized at the expense of the urban poor. As vulnerability and privilege occupy either side of the justice coin, environmental justice should be about dismantling and reversing both (Argüelles 2021c).

This double injustice of historical neglect and impoverishment on the one hand, and unequally distributed access to newly emerging benefits of sustainability on the other, can affect the same groups as they find themselves entangled in webs of power and privilege that traverse history geographically and socially (see Chapter 5). In a recent study, in seven different neighborhoods with a history of environmental injustice and undergoing processes of urban renewal in the United States and Western Europe, traditional environmental health injustices of exposure to toxicity were reproduced and compounded through new processes of gentrification and displacement, as well as through new risks related to climate change or the reemergence of toxicity, resulting in poor mental and physical health for the most vulnerable and in new patterns of health inequity (Cole et al. 2021).

The case of non-EU immigrants in European cities further illustrates patterns of double injustice. Immigrants, who often come from countries that have contributed the least to climate change while suffering its most severe impacts, find themselves once again unprotected from climate impacts when exposed to multiple types of environmental health risks (such as pollution, limited access to green amenities, etc.) and are poorly represented in decision-making processes over urban sustainability transformations. Designed responses to climate change related to resilience and sustainability often have a negative impact on such groups and reproduce inequalities along lines of race, ethnicity or nationality. These compound impacts are referred to as the "triple injustices of climate change" (Anguelovski et al. 2019a). Research from seven growing cities in South Asia and West Africa with high flows of rural-to-urban immigration also showed that addressing the environmental and health risks already affecting vulnerable and marginalized groups such as immigrants is key to delivering urban sustainability and health targets that uphold strong justice components (Szaboova et al. 2022). In Nigeria, for example, poor migrants were more likely to face water-related sanitation health risks because they were already in a situation of housing and tenure insecurity that made access to sustainable water systems structurally impossible (Ibid.). In sum, underlying inequities in environmental health can be a problem that urban sustainability initiatives both aim to solve and inadvertently perpetuate.

Grassroots action and policy tools

Sustainability has become as much a mainstream approach in the policies of many city governments as a common theme guiding the grassroots activities of civil society groups. Community-based initiatives often embrace environmental principles connected to climate change mitigation and preparedness as they reclaim space in the city and forge a voice in the sociopolitical landscape. Community initiatives can range from sustainable energy schemes to waste-to-reuse regenerative and circular economy projects, biking initiatives and local food networks. In Barcelona, for example, families in the dense Eixample district have created the "Bicibus", a pollution- and transit-reduction initiative with the support of the Municipality that facilitates the right of way on certain streets for kids and parents to collectively ride their bikes to school every Friday. A larger-scale initiative for sustainable and just energy in the broader Catalunya region is a cooperative that jointly purchases energy with a green certificate and invests in generating their own renewable electricity, with more than 75,000 members across Spain in 2021 (Argüelles, Anguelovski, and Dinnie 2017). Whereas the potential of these initiatives for just socioecological transformation is undeniable, the practices and discourses emerging from such projects are not exempt from reproducing their own patterns of exclusion, as they range from more radical, transformational and inclusive approaches, to reformist, neoliberal and even exclusive ones (Ibid.).

These kinds of contradictions can also be observed in other forms of urban sustainability practices, such as in urban agriculture initiatives. Urban gardening has multiple benefits on mental and physical health, allowing participants to cultivate affective relationships with urban nature, fellow farmers and community members. Beyond food security and improved diet, food community networks and gardens in marginalized neighborhoods help to address mental health issues including individual and communal trauma, loneliness and isolation, and a sense of loss (Anguelovski 2014). When applied through a lens of justice, such initiatives can address multiple needs of underprivileged neighborhoods, including access to healthy food. Furthermore, when complemented by programs such as healthy school canteens and farmers' markets, urban agriculture can address poor access to food in a more comprehensive way (Anguelovski 2016a). A common policy approach followed by municipalities, such as in Athens, is to support community groups in obtaining and managing land for the cultivation of food through the temporary licitation of empty spaces. In the case of Athens, however, the temporary allocation of garden lots to family units did not foster collaboration between them. Ultimately, some of the members facing issues of mental health, unemployment and lack of time were not able to maintain their gardens in the long term (Kotsila et al. 2020). With no guarantee for longevity and no assistance for the most vulnerable, a lot of urban gardens struggle to fulfill their social objectives. In the case of Hellenikon in Athens, on the other hand, a guerilla garden setup in the former airport did, in fact, remain inclusive, making a political statement on the garden being a revindication of citizens claiming their right to the city and to urban nature while also facilitating collective decisions over the use and management of the space (Apostolopoulou and Kotsila 2021).

From postindustrial Glasgow to the exclusive sustainable city

Glasgow, Scotland, is a postindustrial city known for its deep-seated health inequities, particularly acute in the East End and in North Glasgow. Public health researchers use the term the "Glasgow effect" (Cowley, Kiely, and Collins 2016) in reference to the excess mortality in Glasgow in comparison to that of other similar postindustrial cities in the United Kingdom. Poor health conditions and low life expectancies especially in the north and east parts of the city have been generated by processes of rapid deindustrialization, urban restructuring and slum clearance up until the 1980s, leading to mass unemployment and large swaths of vacant and derelict land. Indeed, Glasgow has consistently had the highest concentration of vacant and derelict land of any local authority in Scotland, with most of it located in North Glasgow and the East End (Glasgow City Council

2020) and much of it replete with toxins from decades of industrial transgressions. The East End, for example, was the site of heavy industry including J&J White chemical company, Dalmarnock Gas Works and Dalmarnock Power Station, the first in particular leaching chromium IV, cyanides and other heavy metals and chemicals into the land and still a cause of risks in old and new residents (Future Climate Info n.d.). Residents of poor areas are more likely to live close to derelict land, suffer from respiratory disease and cancer or have low-birth-weight infants, in comparison to the rest of Glasgow's population (Maantay 2013).

At the same time, these traditionally more deprived parts of the city are the focus of Glasgow City Council-led regeneration projects that seek to build healthy, sustainable and high-quality places. This includes the transformation of the city's 150-year-old Forth and Clyde Canal into Europe's first "smart canal", which according to Scottish Canals will unlock 110 ha across the north of the city for investment, regeneration and development and pave the way for more than 3,000 homes. A planned pedestrian and cycling "street in the sky" bridge crossing the massive M8 motorway, which since the 1970s has cut the Canal off from the city center, seeks to promote sustainable mobility. The green bridge forms part of the £250 million, 50-ha Sighthill Transformational Regeneration Area, the largest project of its kind in the United Kingdom outside London. While only 20% of new residences are planned as social housing, the remaining 80% will cost buyers approximately £200,000, far more than what deeply impoverished local residents can afford. This suggests that the health and related benefits generated by this decontaminated, sustainable environment will be disproportionately reaped by incoming higher-income residents.

A similar story is unfolding in Glasgow's East End, where investment poured in during the late 2000s as a result of winning the Commonwealth Games bid, leading to the public/private Clyde Gateway partnership. The remediation of vacant and derelict land through a green "infrastructure first" approach has been central to the Clyde Gateway's ambition to create 21,000 new jobs, 10,000 new housing units, 20,000 new residents, 400,000 square meters of business space and £1.5 billion of private sector investment. Yet 80% of all housing constructed so far either is designated for private sale or involves intermediate forms of tenure, with no concrete figures available on the amount of social housing to be built despite the evident need of the deprived social demography of the area (Garcia-Lamarca and Gray 2022). Furthermore, conservative politicians, policy think tanks and the media have insistently conflated the local population of East End with the historic environmental characterizations of the territory East End as redundant, decayed and worse (Gray and Mooney 2011). For now, it is unclear how new regeneration projects both in the East End and in North Glasgow will address the local community's well-documented issues of social marginalization, ill health and poverty and enable them to access the health and socioeconomic benefits of the sustainable city.

Figure 5 Exclusive Access to the Benefits of Urban Sustainability Infrastructure

5 Driver 5

Exclusive access to the benefits of urban sustainability infrastructure

Urban injustice stems from the combination of a legacy of unequal access to the benefits of urban sustainability infrastructure and newer forms of inequalities created or exacerbated by sustainability-branded projects such as parks, gardens, trees, greenways and greenbelts, ecosystem restoration projects, boardwalks, or organic food markets and stores (Figure 5). We argue that the exclusive access to the benefits of such infrastructure is both an enduring and new environmental privilege for white and higher-class residents (Argüelles 2021a; Garcia Lamarca et al. 2021) embedded in the competitive urbanism and green growth dynamics of globalizing cities (Gould and Lewis 2016). Although sustainability-oriented amenities offer economic, ecological, health and social benefits to many (Baró et al. 2014; Triguero-Mas et al. 2015), they have not been shown to reduce socioenvironmental vulnerabilities for historically marginalized residents, including working-class groups, minorities and immigrants—living in mid- to large-size cities. Rather, they can potentially produce Green LULUs, or Green Locally Unwanted Land Uses (Anguelovski 2016b; Anguelovski et al. 2019c), a term used to describe green enclaves for wealthy and racially privileged residents as opposed to secured public goods for all urban residents.

A historic legacy of unequal access to urban sustainability amenities

In the United States and elsewhere, whiter and higher-income residents tend to have access to more green space than historically marginalized groups, who suffer from a scarcity of parks and gardens due to a deep history of private underinvestment, public abandonment, and racial segregation and discrimination (Grove et al. 2018; Rigolon, Browning, and Jennings 2018). Similar inequalities in access to green space have been diagnosed in Europe, including France, Germany, Spain and Australia. In German cities,

DOI: 10.4324/9781003221425-6

the highest income earners (more than 5,000 euros per month) have access, on average, to an additional 11,000 m^2 of urban green space in a 500 m buffer zone around their home in comparison with residents earning less than 1,300 euros per month (Wüstemann, Kalisch, and Kolbe 2017). A 2018 study identified that US cities with higher median incomes and lower percentages of Latino and Non-Hispanic Black residents tend to hold higher quality park systems (Rigolon et al. 2018).

Recent studies also point to a correlation between race/ethnicity and poverty, and poor spatial access to parks and other green spaces (Rigolon, Browning, and Jennings 2018; Connolly and Anguelovski 2021; Calderón-Argelich et al. 2021). For example, cities such as Seattle, Austin and Portland, with consistently high and rapid levels of growth since WWII, exhibit the strongest spatial link over time between increased greening and whiter populations. Meanwhile, cities that during the same period experienced economic and population decline, such as Detroit, Baltimore or Cleveland, or a punctuated growth pattern such as San Francisco, New York and Philadelphia, non-white areas have hosted a uniformly low level of greening and mostly in recent years (Connolly and Anguelovski 2021).

Of all racialized groups, African Americans tend to have the least access to green space, including smaller green spaces that are mostly neglected and ridden with safety issues. The same dynamics hold true for tree coverage, boardwalks, waterfronts, community gardens and nature preserves. Historically, these inequalities were often officially codified in city policy. In Austin, Texas, archival city plans show how segregated spaces were created for Black residents in areas that were underserved with parks (Busch 2017). In the early twentieth century, neighborhood housing associations in the United States also put in place restrictive covenants and supported segregation ordinances that attributed certain properties to white homeowners and helped to plant trees in high-income, white neighborhoods, a dynamic well illustrated in Baltimore to date (Boone et al. 2010). Similarly, in Milwaukee, associations managed to leverage funding for urban reforestation programs exclusively toward owner-occupied, higher-income, white urban neighborhoods. Overall, residential segregation has long undermined racialized residents' access to urban nature and other sustainability interventions.

Urban green space and street trees are not the only environmental amenities around which segregation and discrimination were practiced. During the late nineteenth century, in Asbury Park, New Jersey, USA, business owners with the support of local officials used economic growth as a justification for preventing Black residents from freely accessing waterfront boardwalks. By the second half of the 1890s, business owners had largely managed to segregate most public spaces in Asbury Park. The exclusion of Black people from public areas of consumption and leisure was further codified by signs that explicitly barred them from beach pavilions, even those that worked there (Eisenhauer 2021). As a result, many racialized minorities up until today still have a traumatic relationship with nature and green space that they subconsciously or consciously perceive as an uneasy space (Finney 2014). The predominance of white discourses and practices regarding what nature is and who it is for continues to create oppressive and traumatic experiences for racialized residents (Byrne 2012; Anguelovski et al. 2020).

In this regard, exclusive access to the benefits of urban sustainability is defined not only by placement or proximity but also by what formal rules and memories define the usage of such infrastructure and its associated benefits. Exclusion can thus be related to past or present experiences of verbal or physical violence, and consequently fear, as typically experienced by women and non-cisgender people in public (green) spaces (Linander et al. 2019). Such violence relates both to explicit sexist behaviors and to implicit ones born from an urban model and use of space typically centered on masculinity, economic productivity and whiteness which excludes other identities and activities that revolve around care, enjoyment, leisure and informality, as denounced by organizations such as Collectiu Punt6 in Barcelona, and which can be traced back to the gendered ideas of the nineteenth century and its strict distinctions between the home as the private space for women, and the public space as the economic arena exclusive to men. This may explain why today, in general, women do not feel as comfortable in public and green space as men. Women also mostly cycle for recreation and not as commuters, and do so mostly in cities with well-developed cycling infrastructure (Garrard, Handy, and Dill 2012)—a significant trend worth noting when designing for inclusive and sustainable cities.

However, the relationship between greening and inequality is not always linear nor simply about spatial access. Postwar segregation practices in the United States, which mostly saw whites moving out of city centers, meant that Black residents who moved to formerly white neighborhoods inherited many central green spaces. In many cities like Philadelphia or Baltimore, these spaces were still underfunded and included mostly smaller and more crowded parks. In Berlin, the transformation of the former Tempelhof airport into a large public park has not attracted immigrant minorities who seem to underuse the park in comparison with other social groups. Similar dynamics have been identified in Amsterdam in the limited use of the new Amsterdam Noord Noorderpark by racialized minorities (Pérez del Pulgar, 2021). All in all, the exclusion and policing of racialized groups from public and green spaces further compounds environmental injustices, with multiple forms of violence affecting immigrants and minorities that have been denounced by the Black Lives Matter and other anti-racist EJ movements (Pellow 2016).

In short, long-term exclusionary processes embedded in the spatial development of cities and in the political economy underpinning such development explain long-standing environmental inequalities and the exclusionary benefits of urban sustainability infrastructure.

The emergence of the "green space" paradox and how green gentrification sustains the urban green growth machine

Unequal access to green space also overlaps with what some have recently called a green space paradox (Connolly 2018; Gould and Lewis 2016). Rather than creating inclusive access to urban nature, public space or climate-protective infrastructure over the mid or long term, greening projects—especially since the 2000s—are leading to land speculation, large-scale real estate (re)development, increasing housing prices and ultimately the displacement of socially vulnerable residents through a process called ecological gentrification, green gentrification, environmental gentrification or climate gentrification (Gould and Lewis 2016; Anguelovski, Irazábal-Zurita, and Connolly 2019b; Shokry, Connolly, and Anguelovski 2020). Those processes demystify the idea that "green is good" for everyone and every purpose (Angelo 2021).

Some examples in North America include projects such as the New York High Line, and rail-to-trail infrastructures such as the Chicago 6060, the Philadelphia Rail Park and the Atlanta BeltLine. In Atlanta for example, housing values have increased by 18 and 27% between 2011 and 2015 for homes located within 0.8 km of Atlanta's BeltLine greenbelt project (Immergluck and Balan 2018). Green projects also comprise the large-scale clean-up and redevelopment of industrialized waterfronts such as the East Boston waterfront, the Bayview Hunters Point in San Francisco or the Lachine Canal in Montreal (Anguelovski and Connolly 2021). While green resilient infrastructure is meant to protect socially and ecologically vulnerable residents against climate threats and impacts, they instead offer greater security to gentrifying and white residents (Shokry et al. 2020). In Europe, the new green corridors such as Passeig Sant Joan or Carrer Cristobal de Moura in Barcelona, new parks such as Park Central in Valencia and the unequal greening of postindustrial neighborhoods such as The Liberties in Dublin (Kotsila et al. 2020) embody similar dynamics of gentrification and displacement. All in all, these projects illustrate the inner workings of a green growth machine in which investors, developers, planners and high-class residents (Gould and Lewis 2016) benefit from urban greening to the detriment of working-class and racialized residents and their greening traditions, needs and informal spaces.

Moving beyond the Global North, in Asian cities—and South Asia in particular—urban environmental clean-up projects around waterfronts have also caused mass eviction of informal settlers, excluding them from their neighborhoods and from the benefits of new blue and green spaces. This is a process that Ghertner (2010) has termed as "green eviction". In Bangkok, residents have been evicted to give space to newer walkways and bike lanes along the Chao Phraya River. In China, the construction of eco-cities and eco-districts has translated into mass evictions while creating an image of improvement through "green spectacle". Since the 2000s, those large-scale green initiatives have taken place in a broader context of what Ren calls "spectacular urbanism" that promotes Chinese cities in the international arena and attracts new investment.

Research shows that real estate developers are indeed able, in many cities, to leverage rezoning ordinances and tax incentives to redevelop vacant or contaminated land, which they transform into high-end housing complexes next to green spaces (Bunce 2017), and thus contribute to the unequal redevelopment of historically marginalized and underinvested neighborhoods. The exclusive access to the benefits of green space enjoyed by high-income residents is enabled by "green gaps" that municipalities, private investors and privileged residents exploit as "green rent" through new commercial and residential investments associated with greening (Anguelovski and Connolly 2021). Building on Smith's rent gap, the appropriation of green gaps shows how this green growth alliance finds new potential green rents from renaturing projects and formulates them as a win–win scenario that offers benefits and inclusive access to public goods (García-Lamarca et al. 2022). Eventually, real estate developers might also engage in "urban green grabbing"—a process by which they extract additional rent, surplus value, social capital and prestige from locating new residential projects next to new or up-and-coming green amenities—whether or not they build or finance this green space (Ibid.).

Overall, we argue that new environmental inequalities associated with sustainability amenities also arise from the lack of attention paid by planners and elected officials to socioecological vulnerabilities (Shokry et al. 2022) and to mid- and long-term affordability and housing rights issues. As a result, rather than providing ample health and recreational benefits for residents that need them the most, sustainability projects and greening in particular might create "disruptive green landscapes" (Triguero-Mas et al. 2021). These can trigger climate and sustainability planning conundrums, as well as environmental and climate justice challenges (Anguelovski et al. 2020; Gould and Lewis 2016) because of the strong competing economic and financial interests surrounding climate and sustainability initiatives (Sovacool, Linnér, and Goodsite 2015).

Lastly, this unequal access to sustainability amenities also manifests in relation to fresh and affordable food and sustainable food systems. For decades, unequal access to fresh food has permeated the urban landscapes of many underserved neighborhoods (Alkon and Guthman 2017), creating food deserts and undermining healthy food choices for families in lower-income and racialized neighborhoods. At the same time, those neighborhoods historically concentrate a higher number of fast-food restaurants and chains compared to wealthier neighborhoods. Researchers first studied food deserts in the city of Glasgow, Scotland, identifying inequalities structured by class in the availability of food stores, yet also noting that new neighborhood grocery stores with healthier food choices alone did not alter dietary habits in part because of the lasting effect of neighborhood deprivation and derelict land on poor health.

Much like green space, accessibility to fresh and healthy food even today is also subject to gentrification through a process known as food gentrification. Recent research shows that as lower-income neighborhoods see the opening of new supermarkets and organic local food markets, residents often face financial obstacles and sociocultural constraints to purchasing food, experiencing what is known as food mirage, or the illusion of better food access despite very limited access (Sullivan 2014). Moreover, community gardens and urban farms that serve as environmental refugees created by working-class residents are also increasingly "practiced" and "captured" by higher-income residents and thus embedded into gentrification and food injustice dynamics (Maantay and Maroko 2018).

While much of the research on the exclusive access to the benefits of urban sustainability amenities has been conducted in the Global North, Global South cities exhibit similar dynamics of social and spatial exclusion of historically marginalized groups from climate resilient infrastructure, riverfronts and waterfronts, and green space. In Medellin, the construction of the Jardin Circunvalar was envisioned as a green space addressing rapid spatial growth on the hillsides of the city while offering new recreational opportunities and addressing landslides and extreme weather events. Yet it has also been associated with the erasure of residents' informal green space and urban agriculture practices, especially those of internal migrants whose land use is considered an illegal occupation by local planners. At the same time, real estate development on protected land was allowed to move forward in the southern areas of the city of El Poblado, creating what we refer to as "landscapes of pleasure and privilege" for upper-class residents.

Grassroots action and policy tools

Faced with environmental injustices associated with both the legacy of unequal access to green space and green gentrification, historically vulnerable residents and activists are contesting the social effects of greening projects in order to improve access to sustainability amenities and enact justice (Pearsall and Anguelovski 2016; Connolly 2018). Racialized and working-class communities in North America and Europe began organizing in the 1980s for the creation of many new green spaces in historically non-white neighborhoods, and have since then mobilized alliances around them to ensure that empty, underused or contaminated lots become productive, recreational spaces for all residents (Kotsila et al. 2020). As far as green gentrification is concerned, community activists are organizing at the neighborhood and city levels to contest the uneven social impacts of urban greening interventions. Their movement builds on alliances between traditional environmental justice groups and community development organizations that leverage existing environmental policies and regulations meant to protect environmental justice communities from the social impacts of planning schemes, building progressive alliances with gentrifiers and focusing on the right to housing tools (Pearsall and Anguelovski 2016). In other cases, academics work with community groups to document and visibilize green gentrification tensions and conflicts through critical mapping tools.[1]

"Just Green Enough" strategies (Curran and Hamilton 2017) have raised hopes for their combination of contamination clean-up, new greening, and light industry and redevelopment schemes. However, the long-term potential of such green compromises remains to be proven due to risks of community co-optation and demotivation. Key questions remain about alliances between different types of local socioenvironmental movements and organizations. For example, some traditional environmental non-profits do not consider it their business to fight for green equity from a housing perspective and thus fail to make housing rights a priority in their work.

The role of municipal decision-makers and public agencies in addressing or preventing inequities in relation to greening and green gentrification cannot be disregarded. In Atlanta, to address green gentrification around the BeltLine, the city committed to funding new affordable housing through the Tax Allocation District agreement, which will allocate tax revenue from "underutilized" properties in the vicinity of the BeltLine to the BeltLine project. In other cases, cities have passed rent control or rent freeze regulations to keep housing affordable. In Vienna, the Limited Profit Housing Act sets specific guidelines for setting fair rental prices for units developed by private developments. In 2020, Berlin decided to freeze rents at June 2019 levels for the next five years, affecting 90% of the city's apartments and approximately 350,000 residents. In one year, the policy is said to have lowered average rents by 7.8%.[2] In addition, other cities are opening up previously private or privatized green spaces, such as Vogelbuurt Gardens, a then public green space in Amsterdam Noord. Other cities with ambitious green space development plans include Lyon in France, which has prioritized making green spaces accessible along walkable and bikeable corridors, and linking greening with urban transit and mobility, especially in working-class neighborhoods such as La Guillotière (Barcelona Lab for Urban Environmental Justice and Sustainability 2021).

It is clear that many socially vulnerable residents face both the lasting impacts of historic injustices in access to sustainability infrastructure and newer forms of green inequalities born from urban green-grabbing dynamics and the green branding of their long-underinvested neighborhoods. This double dynamic illustrates the need to repoliticize urban greening and urban sustainability more broadly and demystify the notion that green is good (Angelo 2021) for everyone and every purpose in the context of competitive urbanism and green growth dynamics. To move away from urban sustainability infrastructure in the form of GreenLULUs for historically marginalized groups, cities must integrate anti-displacement and anti-gentrification measures into ambitious green space development plans that address the needs of historically marginalized groups. Only through this double prioritization of equity and justice will cities avoid creating and perpetuating green privilege.

Green and food exclusions in Montreal's Saint-Henri neighborhood

The birthplace of Canada's industrial revolution, Montreal's Saint-Henri neighborhood has undergone a significant sociospatial transformation in recent decades, generating popular contestation in terms of who can access the benefits of urban sustainability infrastructures. After decades of neighborhood decline exacerbated in the 1960s by the closure of the Lachine Canal—an important transport site for well over a century—and the construction of the mammoth multilevel Turcot Interchange highway, change began anew in the 1990s. Over $100 million in federal and provincial funds were assigned to decontaminate the Lachine Canal, and many brownfield sites next to it were transformed into creative class commercial spaces and luxury lofts. Since the mid-2000s, the 14-km-long waterway offers one of the best bike paths in Montreal alongside green and blue amenities.

The decontamination of the Canal was a key trigger of a massive building boom, mostly of middle- to high-end residential housing, and also served to rebrand the previously neglected and pejoratively considered area as Les Quartiers du Canal. Many community organizers in Saint-Henri feel that the millions of public sector investments to

improve the Canal, supposedly to the benefit of the existing neighborhood and broader Montreal population, have been seized by private
real estate capital and wealthy residents. The new, expensive housing stands in stark contrast to the unhealthy, poor-quality housing of
long-term working-class neighborhood residents. Furthermore, some
private developments have gated access to the Canal and their own
private docks to access the water. This sparked several community
organizations in the Southwest borough to organize around universal
access to the Canal as a common good. An emblematic pirate action
even took place in 2018 to take over the private docks, denouncing
private real estate and wealthy residents' appropriation of the area.
Also building on a long and rich history of direct action in the neighborhood, there is an ongoing struggle led by community groups to
turn the old Canada Malting Factory on the banks of the Lachine
Canal into social housing.

Just a few blocks north of the Lachine Canal's passage through the
Saint-Henri neighborhood, in the late 2000s the St-Pierre Woonerf
was built, a Dutch "living street" concept for pedestrians, cyclists,
children and general green living. Montreal's Southwest borough
council received $1.5 million from the Quebec Public Health Agency
to create the Woonerf, in the name of combating the heat island effect
and improving the local environment. While social housing exists
along a small portion of the Woonerf, new condo developments boast
their location on the green street. Many requests have been made
for building demolitions, and several properties along the Woonerf
have been converted from multiunit to single-family condominiums.
According to a 2019 article in the National Observer (Keating 2019),
45% of households along the Woonerf have lived there for less than
one year. Local housing and community organizers note that the new
outdoor exercise equipment is largely used by white, middle-class
condo owners, and underline that the local schoolyard play space—
severely in need of investment—currently looks like a prison yard.

This greening and influx of new residents have also transformed
Saint-Henri's foodscape, where new gourmet restaurants and up-scale
cafés, a renovated farmers' market and renovated grocery stores have
displaced the diners, *dépanneurs* (corner stores) and other food shops
long frequented by working-class residents. Today, the neighborhood's
main thoroughfare Notre-Dame Street is lined with brunch restaurants
and cocktail bars, looking nothing like it did just one decade ago. For-
tunately, housing advocacy organizations and community groups have

initiated projects focused on improving food access for lower-income residents through, for example, regular collective kitchen events or organizing vegetable stands in social housing. They also fought for, and won, a new zoning regulation that limits the number of restaurants on Notre-Dame Street to safeguard existing businesses catering to low-income residents and keep commercial rents low.

To date, the struggles for access to the benefits of urban sustainability infrastructure have been won, thanks to the organization and mobilization of Saint-Henri residents. As another large-scale greening project has removed the multilevel highway Turcot Interchange and will integrate a large green space on site, care must be taken to ensure that new exclusions are not created in the process.

Notes

1 See www.bcnuej.org
2 www.dw.com/en/berlins-revolutionary-rent-cap-success-or-flop/a-56664706

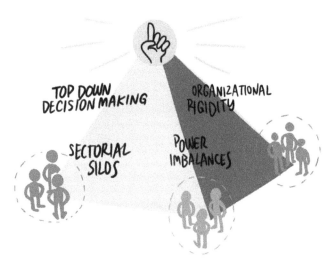

Figure 6 Unfit Institutional Structures

6 Driver 6

Unfit institutional structures

Urban sustainability is heavily dependent on coordinated policy and effective decision-making by urban governance institutions at the local, regional, national and international levels. By institutions, we refer to the more formal structures and mechanisms that govern aspects of social life—from offices, authorities, departments, collectives and organizations to the rules, legal mechanisms and custom practices of official governmental bodies—broadly relating to urban sustainability. In this context, unfit institutional structures as a driver of injustice refer to aspects of urban governance that hinder achieving just urban sustainability processes and outcomes (Figure 6).

One of the most fundamental critiques of high-level public institutions is their adoption of strict top-down approaches, which not only weakens the role of civil society (Chapter 8) but also limits knowledge generation and the emergence of novel solutions to complex problems such as sustainability (Jacob et al. 2019). Moreover, rigid, bureaucratically imposed regulatory barriers often result in approaches to urban sustainability that fail to address the realities of vulnerable residents (Morrow 2019). Another example of unfit institutional structures is the dissonance that occurs between the priorities of municipal and/or regional authorities and those of central (national) government institutions. In recent US history, this is reflected in how the Trump presidency's withdrawal from climate action spurred cities and states to adopt ambitious greenhouse gas emission reduction targets and plans (Jaeger, Cyrs, and Kennedy 2019). National regulatory, legislative or judicial bodies can, in other cases, stand in the way of transformative change at the municipal level, by blocking policy that concerns sustainability indicator monitoring or direct democracy processes (Janoušková 2013; Thompson 2021).

These challenges are underscored by the fact that most existing institutional structures are embedded in or built on historic social relations that have empowered privileged groups (men, white people, property owners) and disenfranchised others (racialized people, women). Throughout history,

DOI: 10.4324/9781003221425-7

the design of Western cities has been led by institutions such as planning offices, municipalities and architectural firms, mainly staffed by cis-male individuals of a certain educational, racial and class background. One of the consequences is they have reproduced the idea that public urban space should primarily serve the functions of production in the formal economy, leaving little room for aspects of care and the informal economy. Moreover, institutions can be unwilling to change existing and long-used methods, metrics or objectives, even as they adopt new discourses to integrate popular buzzwords like "participation" and "sustainability". Despite efforts to transform them, institutional structures and their ingrained power relations tend to dictate distributional patterns and outcomes of urban sustainability initiatives, holding back actions that could benefit vulnerable groups and enhance just urban sustainability (Young 2011). In the example of food sharing across European cities, the SHARECITY project reported that even with recent guidelines established to help increase food donations, "every initiative that handles surplus food, or cooking events, still has to adhere to a policy which was set up primarily for commercial, large-scale operations . . . to take liability and ensure things like the cold chain is maintained" (SHARECITY 2019).

This chapter focuses on two specific aspects driving injustice in urban sustainability initiatives in relation to unfit institutional structures. First is the growing predominance of urban governance in discourse, policy and planning as a way to achieve urban sustainability. This tends to depoliticize complex relationships between actors and avoids questions of conflict that are inherent to society, leading organizations to act in partial, fragmented and disconnected ways that are counterproductive for justice in the context of urban sustainability. Second, the creation of institutional silos and clashing scales and temporalities of action refers to ineffective coordination of complex, intersectoral sustainability issues in ways that exacerbate existing injustices. In the last section, we highlight grassroots actions that can potentially challenge unfit institutional structures through climate adaptation-related experimentation, paying attention to social dissensus, and what new forms of municipalism can do to provide more just, sustainable urban solutions.

Urban governance and the depoliticization of government, politics and conflict

Governance, in its broadest sense, refers to the processes through which complex systems or activities are coordinated; it is about both the formal and informal ways humans manage relationships with each other and their surroundings (Seyle and King 2014). The concept became ubiquitous in international development discourse in the late 1980s, with its (controversial) growth in use reflecting the emergence of multilevel government structures due to the decentralization of governmental roles and responsibilities and the elevation of civil society actors as protagonists (Beall and Fox 2009; Pierre 2011). In the past few decades, the urban scale has been a key terrain for the emergence of new governance arrangements due to innovative social movements and transformations in how governance is conducted (Swyngedouw 2005). Indeed, the spread and importance of the concept are reflected in the global campaign on urban governance launched by UN Habitat (2002) to promote a well-managed, inclusive and sustainable city.

The rise of the governance concept—and its related multistakeholder, public/private partnerships and public/non-profit governance arrangements— has also been linked to urban growth and neoliberalization processes (Chapter 10), with most governance processes fitting hand in glove with the broader neoliberal global (urban) project (Jessop 2002). In the US city of Milwaukee, for example, shared urban environmental governance for urban tree and park provision and maintenance was adopted in the 1990s and 2000s in the context of neoliberalization of urban social service provision, through a transition from state provision to civil sector delivery and a transformation of public agencies into a "shadow state". In fact, between the 1980s and the late 2000s, Milwaukee Parks Department managers fired half of their 400 employees as municipal budgets and the maintenance of trees and parks shrank. At the same time, non-profits such as Greening Milwaukee or Park People of Milwaukee County used unpaid volunteers to protect the tree canopy and manage parks (Perkins 2009). Similar dynamics have been reported in cities such as Philadelphia, where urban park management has shifted toward an entrepreneurial strategy of self-funding through service provision and public/private partnerships (Gabriel 2016).

Governance has also been heavily criticized in theory and practice due to its focus on consensus, its depoliticized approach to policymaking and its neglect of power relations and inequality (Leitner, Peck, and Sheppard 2007). Researchers have uncovered countless cases where urban governance processes mobilize sustainability in a purely discursive fashion to justify urban development and secure public support (Lombardi et al. 2011). This is exemplified in the city of Valencia, Spain, with the redevelopment of an old train infrastructure and the associated creation of a new park, Valencia's Parc Central. The centerpiece of the project, designed through a semi-public governance arrangement involving Spanish national government agencies, public infrastructure companies and the Valencia regional and city level governments, is a high-speed railway infrastructure intervention with a large park ultimately serving as a social and environmental justification (Argüelles 2021a). On the surface, the project appears to tick the "good governance" boxes, but in reality, there was scarce participation from the general public in the conceptualization and realization of the project, which was designed by a renowned architecture firm with an eye to international visibility and city positioning, rather than responding to local transit and green needs (Ibid.).

The fact that different groups have diverging positions and perspectives on urban sustainability interventions is an inherent part of urban social life, yet governance processes focusing on consensus solutions often foreclose the possibility of conflict and exposure to deep inequalities and injustices. For example, long-term coalitions between local government agencies and private development groups that share decision-making and financing power in urban governance structures can have priorities that conflict with those of local communities or can overlook the needs and capacities of historically underinvested neighborhoods. Such conflicts are shaped in part by the historical role of the city as a growth machine (Molotch 1976) and long-standing power imbalances which result in the lack of consideration of marginalized residents' needs and demands in municipal decisions. Even when participatory processes exist within these governance processes, they are often characterized by exclusive outcomes (Fainstein 2014), as explained in detail in Chapter 8. In Glasgow, this is reflected in how new housing developments form part of the broader regeneration of areas surrounding North Glasgow's Forth and Clyde Canal. Several public consultations led by the city council have taken place, yet participation was largely regarded as tokenistic and limited to residents placing sticky notes on plans (Garcia-Lamarca and Gray 2020). In the end, participation processes are limited to a specific project frame, rather than enabling dramatic rethinking of an entire area, indicating how new ideas must be aligned with the interests and plans of existing governance alignments. As a result, rather than providing new social housing and revitalized open space for the most needful residents, redevelopment further anchors social exclusion and inequality.

Nevertheless, the integration of civil society into urban governance processes related to sustainability can have some positive social and environmental results (Frantzeskaki et al. 2016) despite an overall mixed outcome (see also Chapter 8). Initiatives led by civil society—defined as grassroots and community-based organizations, advocacy groups and coalitions that are autonomous from the state—can drive the creation of new social relations and practices. But they can also serve as a convenient way to fill the void left by a retreating welfare state in the name of responsible governance (Ibid.). For example, Bristol, England, was the EU European Green Capital in 2015, thanks in large part to decades of activism by local environmental movements. Yet a 66% decrease in the parks budget from 2013 to 2019 forced Bristol City Council to find revenue-generating schemes to maintain green space and pushed park maintenance and stewardship onto the shoulders of more than 70 community groups across the city (Matheney et al. 2021). Although in theory this scheme was also meant to benefit the more green-deprived neighborhoods, results have been mixed: wealthier neighborhoods have been able to benefit from better maintained green spaces while poorer areas are not *as* capable of undertaking the required level of volunteer work and stewardship (Ibid.). Similar dynamics of social and racial exclusion resulting from the management of urban green space are reported in our example of Milwaukee above (Perkins 2009). Linked to processes of neoliberal urbanism (Chapter 11), this shows how as urban governance expands to spheres beyond the state, the outcomes produced by already existing unfit institutional structures—exemplified here by Bristol City Council's management of parks and green space—can be reinforced or even exacerbated.

Institutional silos and clashing scales and temporalities of action

It is broadly recognized that urban sustainability challenges are "wicked problems" (Rittel and Webber 1973) that require thinking across established boundaries of knowledge and practice. Yet the fact that many of the institutions involved in urban governance work in silos, especially government institutions at multiple scales, inhibits meaningful coordination across issues and boundaries. A silo is a sectoral division created to manage and simplify decision-making on specific tasks or topics, characterized by a specific institutional logic, way of working and culture that inhibits cross-sectoral work (Oseland 2019). In practice, this means that different branches of government at different levels (or even the same), often pursue competing goals (Jacob et al. 2019). In Barcelona, Spain, the creation of a green corridor in the central and dense district of Eixample has been controversial. Framed under a narrative of renaturalization and green climate adaptation, the project allocated a large part of urban public space to new food and drinks businesses, displacing stores owned mainly by people with an immigrant Chinese background. While the municipal urban ecology department at the time (2009–2015) might have responded to local economic regeneration priorities, no housing or other departments were involved to ensure just outcomes for the most vulnerable residents and business owners who were not part of the decision-making process in this sustainability-driven intervention (Kotsila, Anguelovski et al. 2021). Nonetheless, effective mechanisms for cross-silo interaction are needed to effectively ensure coherence in actions to implement the UN Sustainable Development Goals and the 2015 Paris Agreement on climate change (Adams and Judd 2016).

The question of scale in relation to unfit institutional structures further not only complicates the drivers of injustice in urban sustainability but also provides a possibility for transformation. Scale is a widely used geographic term often used in a static way to identify local, regional or global levels (to name a few) of policy, action or planning. Here, rather, we understand scale as a process that is socially produced and a result of social struggles for power and control, and as such, one that can be contested and restructured (Swyngedouw 1997). Responses to climate change provide a good example of scales that are clashing and subject to reconfiguration. International policy discourse long-presented climate change as a global problem requiring global solutions, a framing which tended to focus on the nation-state and neglected other scales of decision-making that also shape potential responses and ways to act (Bulkeley and Newell 2015). A focus on climate governance at the urban scale has emerged in response to this global agenda, signaling a shift or contestation in political authority and the political economy of carbon (Bulkeley, Castán Broto, and Edwards 2015).

In Surat, India, for example, local governments that operate without a comprehensive planning framework for climate adaptation but that still wish to pursue climate adaptation efforts have managed to switch between different types of financial flows, intergovernmental fiscal transfers and municipal revenues to sustain action. Surat has managed to identify adaptation and development co-benefits and exploit this synergy to fund climate adaptation through projects already funded by existing and forthcoming streams of public revenue (Cook and Chu 2018). This way, adaptation is integrated into urban development planning, prioritized alongside development needs and through options co-created among public and civic actors (Chu 2016). The municipality of Surat has also been supported since 2012 by the Surat Climate Change Trust, a multistakeholder group tasked with making the adaptation agenda more durable, seeking additional funding for key urban sectors such as waste and sanitation, water management or affordable housing, and redirecting funding for adaptation purposes to the city's most vulnerable groups (Chu, Anguelovski, and Carmin 2015).

Finally, differing temporalities can further exacerbate the lack of fit institutions addressing sustainability and justice. Most public and private institutional actors tend to work on shorter time frames, driven by efficiency and productivity-oriented goals. This has been framed by researchers as "event-driven" time frames, reflected in the time needed for construction schemes or redevelopment milestones (Moore-Cherry and Bonnin 2020). When planning and implementing urban sustainability interventions, this short-term time scale can clash with the temporalities of other groups and with the lived experience of the city. For example, municipal planners implementing car-free zones across Bergen, Norway face trade-offs between longer time frames required to build sufficient knowledge and deeply engage with other urban governance actors and impending project deadlines (Sareen et al. 2021). The first car-free zone—established in the central neighborhood of Møhlenpris with a history of resistance to car-based development—experienced ease in positively engaging with organized neighborhood groups to govern the intervention, despite the distinct historical materialities and social practices that urban planners expected would present significant challenges in the suburbs (Ibid.). Such clashing temporalities determine the transformative and justice potentials of sustainability mobility interventions that seek to make the city more just and sustainable.

Grassroots action and policy tools

Despite the challenges of unfit institutional structures and their related governance processes, positive change is possible. Youth involvement, for example, has been fundamental in ensuring inclusive adaptation planning in Quito, Ecuador. At the start of the process, youth support was galvanized through the Youth National Convention on Climate Change in the late 2000s, where youth groups across Ecuador adopted a climate action platform and proposed a list of youth-relevant policy recommendations for municipal departments (Chu, Anguelovski, and Carmin 2015). Youth participation in climate planning also translated into neighborhood climate risk awareness campaigns, local debates on municipal climate policies championed by youth and their voice being integrated into policy input and project implementation. Also providing hope are the growing number of urban climate change experiments, which make it possible to reconfigure unjust governance structures and processes and provide legitimacy to new sociotechnological configurations (Bulkeley, Castán Broto, and Edwards 2015).

Building on experimentation, the idea of new municipalism in the past five years has gained ground, exemplified by leftist coalitions in the local government proposing a dramatic democratization of cities. New or "radical" municipalism efforts seek to overcome unfit institutional structures by focusing on local-scale action as a lever against austerity and as the site for the transformation of state and capitalist social relations (Thompson 2021). While not unproblematic, this scale of action has brought much inspiration in terms of making more just and sustainable cities. Finally, rather than focus on consensus-building in urban government, cities may find that monitoring social dissensus and disagreement can shed light on the various dimensions of unfit institutional structures and help us to radically change institutional practices and frameworks by genuinely integrating excluded groups as co-decision-makers (Kaika 2017).

Clashing temporalities of social community gardening and municipal institutional frameworks in Barcelona

During a time of economic crisis, back in 2012, austerity cuts and a stall in investments had left several unused empty plots of land lying idle around the city of Barcelona. Led by Mayor Trias, the municipal government in power at the time adopted the *Pla Buits* (Vacant lots Plan), in order to place such unused municipal land at the service of civil and non-for-profit groups. Citizens were encouraged to develop and propose plans for the temporary (three-year) development of activities that would strengthen social cohesion in their neighborhood.

Barcelona has historically faced a deficit of public green space compared to other EU cities and has gone through a decade (2000s–early 2010s) of private sector and investment-oriented urban green politics leading to inequities in green space distribution, green gentrification impacts and the creation of green enclaves (Anguelovski et al. 2018; Kotsila et al. 2021). In this context, the great demand for more equitable, proximate and participatory green spaces for the community was expressed in the large percentage of urban gardening projects proposed for the Pla Buits program (9 out of the 14 projects that were selected during the 2012–2015 implementation period), building on a legacy of community organizing around public green spaces throughout Barcelona. Among those was the *Illa dels 3 horts* (Island of three gardens), a plot of land converted into an urban gardening project located in the Sants-Montjuic district, in close vicinity to exhibition centers, museums and tourist attractions around Plaça Espanya, in the center of Barcelona.

The project was initiated by a non-for-profit cooperative working to support individuals with unequal opportunities (ex-convicts, people at risk of social exclusion and people with mental health problems), offering a space where they can connect to each other, to the neighborhood and to urban nature. However, it proved hard to engage vulnerable individuals who were facing social exclusion and stigmatization and who were finding it hard to dedicate their time and energy. At a certain point, in 2013, the project risked being abandoned, but a group of local families volunteered to become the main stewards while maintaining it as a space of support for the implicated cooperative and its members. Despite its original short-term life expectancy, the garden still functions as of 2022, yet more as an outdoor social center than a food cultivation plot. The small production of vegetables is shared and used as an input for community meals and events. The garden serves as a space where families from the neighborhood can go for recreation and bonding, cultivating environmental and food consciousness, as well as integrating vulnerable members of the local community.

Through its long-lasting success as a project, as well as through the organizational "crisis" it underwent during its implementation, *Illa dels 3 horts* highlights the importance of the slow and deeper process of creating a garden—and a community around it—which eventually is what also cultivates its social benefits. While the municipal authorities had offered the land and some basic materials (seeds, tools and water provision) necessary to create the garden, the equally necessary physical and emotional labors received less attention and appreciation. Our research shows that the assumption that citizens and communities will always have such resources in abundance and can promptly mobilize them in grassroots sustainability projects, like urban gardens, stems from an institutionalized mentality where activities away from the formal economy and productive sphere, such as caring for others and the environment, remain unpaid, invisible, misunderstood and unaccounted for, while they are also in opposition with legally imposed time frames (Kotsila et al. 2020).

During the life of the program, *Pla Buits* projects were assessed mostly on the quantifiable aspects of success in implementation, such as the participation of people from the wider community (the number of people involved, people visiting, social media presence, etc.). However, the more intangible benefits that build on the everyday materialities of care for urban socionatures (such as inclusive placemaking, breaking stereotypes, horizontal organizing and problem-solving toward just outcomes, etc.), and which often need more time to emerge, were either taken for granted or brushed aside. More importantly, the temporality of programs such as *Pla Buits* reflects a short-term horizon of support within a broader neoliberal premise of prioritizing growth-promising uses of urban space, as well as shifting environmental justice responsibilities to individual citizens (Kotsila, Anguelovski et al. 2021). When, for example, funds become available for real estate development and new construction, the municipality can assign a different use to the plot that used to serve as a community garden, without a guarantee that a replacement can be found. Whereas the piece of land where *Ila dels 3 horts* stands is officially designated as "green zone" according to local zoning laws, and thus relatively protected from eviction, other community gardens in the city are not. In fact, activists have criticized the Pla Buits policy as depoliticizing ongoing struggles from local movements to reclaim urban space and the right to the city (2011–2015), including via the occupation of empty lots toward guerilla gardens with a long-term horizon (Ibid.).

With a shift in urban governmental politics since 2015, the city of Barcelona today puts a strong emphasis on equitable access to green space and on small scale, informal greening along with other climate change adaptation and mitigation measures, with closer attention to the needs of vulnerable social groups and disinvested neighborhoods, encouraging and putting in practice participatory planning and civil engagement in city making (Barcelona City Council 2013, 2018). Nevertheless, in a broader context of real estate speculation and dense urban development, and the often-clashing temporalities between community-based practices and urban governance frameworks, community gardens continue to face precarity, putting their social and ecological benefits at risk.

Figure 7 Weakened Civil Society

7 Driver 7

Weakened civil society

The term "civil society" encompasses a multitude of organizational formats, including grassroots and community-based organizations, advocacy groups, NGOs, coalitions and professional associations. These normally are, or aspire to be, institutionally separate from the state and the market (Frantzeskaki et al. 2016). But among them, the differences in stakeholder profiles and range of operational structures and fields are vast. Although we refer to civil society in singular, it is problematic, if not impossible, to perceive it as a single uniform body of actors. Civil actors, depending on their context, can have diverse and even conflicting needs, rationales and imaginaries (Sekulova, Kallis, and Schneider 2017). Beyond attempts to arrive at a strict definition of the term and its sociological breadth, here we aim to unpack its meaning and manifestation in relation to (in)justice in the context of urban sustainability. The basic premise is that when justice is compromised due to authoritarian, repressive or undemocratic state government regimes, or rent-seeking organizations or actors, it is commonly civil society that unveils and mobilizes responses to issues of social discrimination and exclusion. A weakened civil society, then, is likely to result in the reproduction and even normalization of discriminatory and oppressive acts and processes—from dispossession to misconduct—on the part of public or private actors who are not held accountable (Figure 7). Therefore, the functioning of civil society in relation to urban space is tightly linked to procedural and intersectional forms of justice and the way diverse identities and cultures are represented and recognized in decision-making processes around sustainability (Anguelovski et al. 2020).

Relatedly, and like "citizen participation" (see Chapter 9), the term civil society can often be misinterpreted, manipulated or co-opted. For example, the "involvement of civil society" in policymaking can be a way of virtuously glossing over policies that rollback state welfare, through mass privatizations, or eliminating essential provisioning, such as support toward

DOI: 10.4324/9781003221425-8

local socioecological transitions to sustainability, and shifting increasingly important responsibilities onto citizens (Jeffrey, Staeheli, and Marshall 2018). A growing body of literature, therefore, addresses the importance of the "uncivil" or the "disobedient" in civil society (Scherhaufer et al. 2021). Acts of civil disobedience—such as breaking into a coal mine or blocking a road to demand environmental justice—reflect the discursive and material processes of social change and the existence of fundamental disagreements on the core tenets of urbanization, climate and energy politics, among others. Such disagreements cannot be easily brushed aside by mere improvements in planning or governance processes, and a tokenistic participation of selected stakeholders or civil society representatives, which deny sustainability of "a space of contestation and agonistic engagement" (Ibid.; Wilson and Swyngedouw 2015, 6).

Weak civil society: drivers and tensions

Civil society is assumed to play a fundamental role in sustainability transitions, democratization and civil emancipation in general. Research from a wealth of European case studies on community-led sustainability initiatives finds that civil society organizations can be a driver of sustainability transitions while operating to service social needs within communities that have been neglected or abandoned by the state and the market (Frantzeskaki et al. 2016). Civil society groups in the Global North have also been able to provide a powerful counterbalance to the pervasive effects of neoliberal policies, sustaining democratic processes and embracing intersectional differences (Chu, Anguelovski, and Carmin 2015). Some of the key factors that directly or indirectly undermine and disempower civil society relate to three main areas: funding sources, prohibitive institutional framework and vested economic interests.

Extreme dependence on donor funding can disempower and force particular strands of civil society to minimize or adapt their objectives, eventually diminishing their political relevance (Herz 2016). Often, the time and effort of those on the front lines of justice struggles remain poorly compensated, making these struggles difficult to sustain. Alternatively, many well-intentioned civil society organizations find themselves on a "grant-seeking treadmill", jumping from one short-term project to another, and sometimes circumventing their longer-term visions around sustainability and justice (Johnson and Saarinen 2011). The Huntly and District Development Trust in Scotland, dedicated to the promotion of local sustainability, for example, was forced to prioritize projects that offered economic return over others that may have aligned better with their initial mission (Sekulova et al. 2016b).

Next, experiencing a prohibitive political and institutional environment is a fundamental factor that weakens the role and function of civil society. An extreme, though lucid, example is the modification of the NGO law as of 2006 in Russia which gave legal rights to the Justice Ministry to monitor, and hence sanction, civil society groups that are not seen as supportive of President Putin's power (Johnson and Saarinen 2011). Such acts automatically ousted groups that tended to speak out in defense of environmental justice. Belarus is another extreme case where civil society's views on the way urban green and blue spaces are being transformed are heavily censored (Kronenberg et al. 2020). A large civil society is not necessarily a robust and emancipatory one. Under the rule of the "Justice and Development Party" in Turkey—and its weak democratic credentials—civil society grew in size and functionality. The authoritarian regime appropriated civil society by encouraging those in support of the regime and repressing any antagonistic movements. Emancipatory forms of civil organizing, as spaces of dissent and resistance to the dominant paradigms of an authoritarian regime, were gradually disabled and marginalized (Yabanci 2019).

Vested economic interests are another major factor that weakens civil society's struggles for urban sustainability and justice. Community and solidarity gardening projects that emerge on abandoned urban terrains when the cost of land is relatively low are particularly vulnerable to eradication and displacement the moment powerful economic players reclaim the space. Meanwhile, urban community gardens thrive on visible and invisible care work. From soil conditioning and plant growing to mutual learning and self-organization, defending space or relocating, urban gardens offer places of connection and meaning for all (Kotsila et al. 2020). The Druzhba Solidarity Garden in Sofia (Bulgaria), functional between 2011 and 2021, provided a space for cultivating and growing food for those in need. Owned by a mix of municipal and private actors, the land had been occupied in a semi-legal fashion by approximately 100 local gardeners from a nearby green-deprived working-class neighborhood. Financially maintained through donations, the garden provided emotional asylum (Anguelovski 2014) and a space for learning and contact with the soil for hundreds of citizens, especially the elderly, without any form of public support. In the fall of 2021 and without prior notice, construction equipment appeared on the garden premises. In the words of a gardener:

> [W]e were told to move out. They refused to even give me a phone number, or a name, of the landowners to understand what was going on. In the last six months, different people have tried to talk with the municipality to no avail. Not that I attach that much importance to this garden, but this place gave me solace and made me happy. Not just

me, but another 100–150 people. In times of the pandemic, this was an environmental, social, and cohesive effort.

In the case of La Vanguardia community garden in Barcelona, its prospective demolition was communicated well in advance. In 2016, a group of citizens demonstrating against mass tourism in the neighborhood of Poblenou squatted a municipal area sandwiched between the construction sites of two hotels. The terrain was transformed into one of the largest community gardens in Poblenou. Through this action, residents not only reclaimed unused public land but also introduced a new "commons", a place for neighbors to gather, plant and socialize. Unfortunately, in 2020, after the completion of the nearby hotels and several public hearings, the garden was bulldozed to make way for a more "aesthetic" and tourist-friendly front lawn for the hotel Voraport. Both these urban gardens where civil society mobilizes around issues of urban nature, land accessibility, social cohesion and the "right to the city" resulted in collectively shaped versions of nature and sustainability, where nature had been socially constructed and negotiated (Swyngedouw 2007). Yet without legal, judicial or state support, such forms of socionatures can hardly stand the pressure of the economic and financial interests of the day.

The vicious circle of weak civil society, weak sustainability and weak social justice

On the one hand, when civil society is weak, the societal uptake and push for equitably distributed sustainability initiatives and green infrastructure are low or non-existent. Framing sustainability initiatives too narrowly can, on the other hand, debilitate and disallow the participation of more vulnerable social groups. The challenges faced by civil society can be an indicator of the extent to which environmental justice may end up on the agenda of public institutions that work around questions of sustainability. In other words, when civil society is weakened, sustainability policies and projects can undermine social justice.

One example is the practice of fencing urban green and blue infrastructure in several Russian cities, where civil mobilization around issues of social equity and inclusion is relatively weak. A group of urban environmental justice researchers reported that the enclosure of (semi-private) residential backyards, recreational zones and pedestrian pathways has become a common practice (Kronenberg et al. 2020). Local green and blue infrastructure is thus turning into a mosaic of fragmented, disconnected and inaccessible spaces (Ibid.). Exclusionary practices are especially visible in the waterfront areas of Moscow where plots of land are being acquired by officials and the oligarchs who privatize, build up and block communal access to water, despite national decrees that safeguard its universal (public) accessibility. Likewise, the urban parks and forests across many districts in St. Petersburg are facing a continuous threat of construction. Citizen groups there have been confronting the connivance of municipal authorities that favor the interests of construction companies over the equitable distribution of green infrastructure. In the words of local activists, the systematic urban encroachment of parks and forests in St. Petersburg is turning the city into a "stone jungle" for ordinary citizens (Gradozashtnyi Petersburg 2019).

Radicality in grassroots civil mobilization does not imply diversity of representation. Activists and campaigners around climate justice in the Global North are frequently homogeneous in age, economic background and values (de Moor 2018). Strong civil society mobilization around sustainability transitions—frequently represented by white, well-educated individuals—may be associated with low awareness of such networks on intersectional inequalities related to race, ethnicity or migrant background (Argüelles et al. 2017). A study on a range of small-scale and community-based initiatives around organic food, renewable energy and recycling across Finland, Germany, Scotland, Italy and Spain found that the social inequality dimension of sustainability was not given as much priority as its spatial and ecological counterpart. In interviews, many participants acknowledged the pervasiveness of social inequality and injustice but felt inept and incapable of profoundly and effectively addressing them (Sekulova et al. 2016b).

In the field of sustainable food, neoliberal structures privilege productivism and large-scale food producers, making organic food inaccessible to low-income fractions of the population (Argüelles et al. 2018). In this context, organic food cooperatives face significant economic barriers, which is one of the factors that foreclose ethnic and class diversity in their membership. Language, cultural codes and prior specific knowledge can also act as exclusionary factors for joining such sustainability initiatives. Multilingual societies and neighborhoods may fail to meaningfully include linguistic minorities and disadvantaged groups in sustainability initiatives that involve deliberation, as seen in the case of food-sharing experiments in Berlin, Germany. There, language restrictions have limited the sense of multicultural ownership and accessibility of such programs (Morrow 2019). Addressing uniformity in civil society membership, however, need not mean transferring the responsibility for "fixing injustices" onto civil society actors alone, as in the context of roll-out neoliberalism (Peck and Tickell 2002). The ubiquitous structural inequalities in which community-based organizations are embedded show why the accessibility of sustainable food, transport, housing and energy, for example, needs also to be addressed at the macro level, through actions like strong redistributive public policies, progressive wealth taxation and polluter-pay schemes.

As discussed in Chapter 9 on citizen participation, engaging in grass-roots initiatives around sustainability or in socioenvironmental struggles (e.g., around housing, or right to the city) is time- and energy-intensive for those who are financially strained, or have a disproportionate load of care responsibilities to attend to (Sekulova et al. 2016a). In contexts of extreme economic precarity, struggles around urban resilience and renewable energy may seem too demanding and thus less compelling. This can create the false impression that sustainability issues are not of relevance to disenfranchised civil groups, or that sustainability does not speak to the needs of these groups. Urban climate resilience, however, is more important for those living in risky, and typically less attractive areas that are prone to flooding, landslides or excessive heat exposure. Research in the context of climate-related extreme events indicates that the most vulnerable pockets of the urban population tend to be disproportionately affected (Anguelovski et al. 2019a). As stated in the chapter on limited citizen participation, cities must engage directly with vulnerable communities—people of color, low-income groups, single parents and ethnic minorities—and place their material and immaterial needs at the center of policymaking.

Grassroots action and policy tools

Often, community-based initiatives concerned with the struggles of marginalized groups in multicultural neighborhoods tend to have higher chances of enhancing environmental justice, not least locally (Sekulova et al. 2016a). These observations originate from the European research project TESS, which explored a wide range of grassroots initiatives in the field of sustainability between 2013 and 2016 across Europe. Results pointed to community-based bike-repair shops as some of the most socially inclusive sustainability initiatives, with two examples being the initiatives Ciclonauti (Rome, Italy) and Biciosxs (Barcelona, Spain), both aimed at encouraging cycling as an affordable means of transport in the city. Ciclonauti launched in 2000 with the support of the Critical Mass civil disobedience and bicycle street blockade movement pointing to the rights of non-motorized means of being in the urban domain. Biciosxs started out by squatting an abandoned industrial shed in a working-class district of Barcelona in 2005. In both cases, cycling is a common attraction around which people come together to critically reflect on societal structures, discussing issues of transport and social justice. Over time, Ciclonauti engaged in a wide array of social projects, working with homeless people, hosting arts and crafts workshops with individuals with physically diverse abilities and organizing tandem cycling for blind people, among others. Both provided access to low-income individuals. Biciosxs did not charge money for their bike-repair support, instead accepted barter or donations in the form of tools, repair material or food, which made their space welcoming for low-income migrant residents. Overall, both initiatives achieved a multifunctional space, which was not only about repairing bicycles but also served as a community gathering space, combining sustainability with social inclusion.

A relevant question that remains and deserves further discussion, however, is which civil society groups need the most support, or visibility, in the context of environmental and social injustice. One example of tackling systemic poverty, violence and unhealthy lifestyles among indigenous communities in Winnipeg (Canada) is the urban gardens and healing spaces initiated by the Spence Neighborhood Association and the West Broadway Community Organization (Katona 2018). One of these is the Chief Grizzly Bear's Garden in the deprived Spence neighborhood of Winnipeg, which aims to increase the visibility of the large aboriginal population in the area by offering a ceremonial space, honoring the land and cultivating indigenous plants and medical practices (Ibid.). Furthermore, the Grandmothers Healing Lodge, in the same context as Winnipeg, initiated by an indigenous female elder, gives support to (indigenous) women who have suffered trauma, sexual trafficking and violence (Ibid.), working also to preserve ancestral practices.

While the examples in this chapter are intentionally scant, diverse and incomparable, they aim to illustrate distinct realities where struggles for social justice can ground sustainability endeavors and demonstrate that sustainability is inconceivable without social justice and vice versa. Often, sustainability in urban regeneration is seen and measured in narrow and technical terms relating to single domains such as energy efficiency or carbon-neutrality, or superficially characteristic of being green or "nature-like" by focusing on proximity (thus distribution), but not on other aspects of justice related to urban nature (Anguelovski et al. 2020). We have discussed elsewhere in the book what the implications of such narrow sustainability metrics are in terms of perpetuating and deepening material inequalities, ethnically exclusionary urbanization, uneven urban regeneration and health landscapes. The role of civil mobilization here is fundamental in uncovering injustice and fighting against unfit institutional arrangements and the mantra of eternal neoliberal economic growth (D'Alisa et al. 2014). Many authentic acts and transformational paths to binding justice with sustainability are often found on the margins of societal organizing and remain on the fringe of society (Hanáček et al. 2020). These "just sustainabilities" are already enacted in the peripheries of civil society, but need to be acknowledged, supported and used as a source of inspiration for an authentically just sustainability transition.

The politics of real estate pressure in green areas of Mladost, Sofia

One emblematic case of weakening civil society in public planning is manifested in the conflict around the progressive erasure of green areas and children's playgrounds in the working-class Mladost district in Sofia, Bulgaria. The district has a typical socialist design, with multistory blocks separated by ample green fields. Mladost is one of the largest districts in the city, and one deprived of urban parks. Furthermore, the green areas in between its apartment blocks are poorly maintained, deprived of typical elements such as flowers, ornamental trees, blue spaces or alleys. Nevertheless, they have played and still play a key role as spaces for socializing, children's playgrounds, resting and even guerrilla gardening.

As a result of the restitution process in Bulgaria, where land previously confiscated by the socialist state was returned to its owners, many of the green fields in the Mladost district became private property. As a result, construction pressure in most districts of the city skyrocketed. Multiple green fields between the apartment blocks in Mladost have been slowly disappearing, making the district one of the densest in town. Most of the new buildings constructed or planned for construction were high-end residential developments or shopping centers.

In 2016, a small group of citizens organized a spontaneous protest upon seeing the children's playground in front of their housing block fenced off for construction. Eventually, their protesting actions attracted many other residents experiencing similar construction pressure in the district. After multiple mobilizations and public appeals, citizens formed the association "Together for Mladost" to campaign for the protection of the inter-block green areas and the neighborhood commons.

> "Despite our mobilizations, the public administration of Sofia city kept issuing permits and legalizing huge construction projects, while green areas and inter-block spaces were being built up and destroyed one by one. Our living space was literally disappearing in front of our eyes, air quality indicators were deteriorating, and congestion was increasing, as were fights for parking spaces"—[extract of a declaration by the neighborhood association "Together for Mladost", 27/05/2021].

According to the neighborhood association, construction works were indiscriminate and widespread, initiated without public discussion or consultation. At the same time, the newly built blocks and entire subneighborhood enclaves, including closed luxury residential complexes, were not accompanied by the development of new schools or kindergartens, creating a significant shortage of schools in the area.

The committee campaigned for limiting the construction boom in the district without much success until one of its members ran for local election (2016) and won to become mayor of the Mladost district. Desislava Ivancheva was elected with an outstanding majority as a voice of the civil mobilizations around the green commons.

As the new mayor, Ivancheva filed multiple complaints and attempted to pause multiple developments, many of them led by large-scale real estate companies. In April 2018, upon entering her car together with her deputy, she was surrounded by specialized riot police who "accidentally discovered" a large amount of cash (70,000 euros) in the back seat. Ivancheva and her vice-mayor (Bilyana Petrova) were charged with corruption and given 20 years of prison time. Ivancheva and Petrova say they were framed by construction businesses and local mafia as a fast-track solution to oust them out of power.

Historically, few politicians in Bulgaria have received such hefty charges. In a public declaration, the neighborhood assembly stated that the political clique around the ruling party supported by investors, construction contractors, the property mafia, the prosecutor's office and the court staged a "mind-boggling, spectacular and arrogant arrest" as a way to punish the mayor and vice-mayor of Mladost for their uncompromising behavior with respect to the protection of green areas and municipal lands. The conditions of their arrest were extremely poor, and their sentences—based on dubious testimony and evidence—were obscene and offensive. The two women were absolved and released from prison two years later, after paying a financial charge, which they managed to collect through donations.

Local mobilizations against ongoing construction in Mladost continue, though without much ambition to take state power again, and seemingly diminished public support. The arrest and heavy sentence used to oust social justice activists from a position of power sends out a clear warning to anyone planning to run for elections in defense of the commons in Sofia.

Figure 8 Limited Citizen Participation

8 Driver 8

Limited citizen participation

Citizen participation can be generally defined as the involvement of individuals and communities in public decision-making (Figure 8). Yet the terms "citizen" and "participation" require scrutiny as they are both heterogeneous and generic, and often used together as a catch-all phrase prone to ambiguous interpretations. The notion of "citizen", for example, has often been criticized and contested for being used too narrowly and hence exclusively, in the sense of citizenship as a legally established category.

The first question to address regarding issues of justice in citizen participation in the field of urban planning is: who counts as a citizen? Justice research and moral ethics rest on a wider and more inclusive definition of citizens beyond those who are legally recognized subjects of national states. Citizenship can here be understood more broadly as a place-based form of right and obligation that applies to all members of a territorially defined community, including those whose formal social and economic rights are truncated by state institutions. In other words, all individuals residing in a given urban territory can, and shall, enact (Isin 2000) their rights to participate in processes of urban planning in the city regardless of their juridical status.

The second question concerns participation and its forms, means, levels and boundaries. Civil participation in the urban context can be broadly defined as the process of (re)claiming and defending the "right to the city", or "the right of all inhabitants, present and future, permanent and temporary, to inhabit, use, occupy, produce, govern and enjoy just, inclusive, safe and sustainable cities, villages and human settlements, defined as commons essential to a full and decent life".[1] Conceptualizing and enacting participation too narrowly frequently excludes certain groups and effectively undermines their right to the "city commons". In the context of justice and urban sustainability, civil participation thus requires an explicit definition, or even a shared understanding at the level of the actors that promote, embody and enact it.

DOI: 10.4324/9781003221425-9

A classic reference that continues to frame our understanding of participation is the "ladder" approach conceived by Sherry Arnstein (1969), which conceptualizes citizen involvement as a continuum of non-participation, tokenism and citizen control. In her classification, public consultations ultimately serve as *tokenistic* forms of participation, whereas delegated power, citizen control and partnership offer forms of participation that could enable citizens to wield political influence and exercise the "right to the city". Though the ladder concept originated over years ago and was extensively applied and reworked over time, especially in the field of urban environmental (dis)amenities, it remains as pertinent as ever. In the domain of urban greening, for example, Puskás et al. (2021) show that tokenistic forms of participation based on consultation and placation (along Arnstein's ladder) are those most frequently employed, while delegation and citizen control are relatively rare. In this light, our discussion on limited citizen engagement as a driver of environmental injustice can be framed around three core themes: promoters, partakers and formats of participation.

Participative processes

The motivations and expectations of those who promote participation are hugely important for social justice. The spaces and forms in which citizens are invited to participate are inevitably framed by those who organize such processes (Pretty 1995), which makes us take a closer look and the explicit and implicit ideas that underlie them. Is participation organized in a "tick-the-box" kind of fashion to obtain a layer of moral authority, legitimize predetermined decisions and move projects onto the next phase? Injustice in this context frequently emerges due to pre-set agendas where dissent, conflicting views and confrontation are not appreciated (Kesby 2005). A related consideration is whether the underlying function of participation is *instrumental*, in other words, a governance tool for the purpose of reaching a goal, or *transformative*, that is, an end in and of itself.

A lucid example of *instrumental* (or tokenistic) participation took place around the contested construction of a domestic waste incinerator in the vicinity of several working-class neighborhoods in Sofia (Bulgaria) that would potentially affect the health of millions of residents. Deliberately organized by the city administration during the quieter summer months of 2021, the public discussions were attended by a total of ten people, all of whom were working in close collaboration with the administration. Tokenistic forms of participation that serve to push projects forward despite substantial opposition from diverse civil stakeholders pave the way for injustice and constitute the modus operandi of many centralized public institutions.

Seeking citizen engagement once the project design has been developed is one case of *instrumental* participation. Looking at participation patterns and approaches in six green infrastructure projects in Belgium, the United Kingdom, Germany and the Netherlands, Wilker et al. (2016) report that stakeholders were involved in the late planning stages (i.e., discussing specific design and implementation), but not in the earlier phases of conceptualization and vision.

The crucial role of promoters' initial framing for eventual project results is exemplified by a study of the Poonga project in the southern Indian city of Chennai by Ellis (2011). Meant to restore the Adyar River and its estuary, the project created a sanitized, urban green recreational space that required bulldozing some 500 homes in the working-class neighborhood of Raja Gramanito clear space for the so-called river restoration in a process the author calls "the depoliticisation of the production of urban nature". The initial proposal was met with serious criticism from Indian environmental groups that resulted in court orders and substantial modifications, forcing Poonga's developers to transform the project based on inputs from a selected range of stakeholders, namely, NGOs, consultancy firms, planners and environmental clubs. The result was eventually branded as an innovative model of public participation in environmental restoration and clean-up. The initial framing of Poonga as an element of a competitive growth strategy, where ecological modernization fuels "development-orientated urban natures", was nonetheless never abandoned. Rather, participation was orchestrated by incorporating and legitimizing only those voices and critiques that are compatible with the initial framing (Ibid.).

Participants

Other pertinent questions relating to how limited citizen participation emerges as a driver of injustice are: *Who* participates versus *who* does not, at what stages and with what impacts? The participation of a small group of highly articulate self-appointed community members would differ, for example, from that of delegated community members who engage with the process and report back to the group in a more inclusive and horizontal fashion (Cornwall 2008). The diversity of participants, including their socioeconomic status, ethnicity and cultural background, is key. While participatory processes cannot involve everyone for logistical reasons, finding a balance between participation depth (extensive conversations, sufficiently long time frame) and breadth (variety of representation) is fundamental for the inclusion of diverse views, opinions and interests (Ibid.).

When insufficient time and resources are dedicated to engaging with disenfranchised communities and those most affected by processes of urban change related to sustainability, participation fails to support just outcomes and may even deepen existing inequalities. The communities most vulnerable to gentrification-driven displacement are the ones most impacted by it while having little to no say in the decision-making processes that drive the gentrification in the first place (Anguelovski and Connolly 2021). To make things worse, some experience attempts at coercing their participation, resulting in exasperation, distrust and cynicism (Cornwall 2008). For the most vulnerable parts of the urban population (low-income families, single mothers, immigrants, marginalized minorities, etc.), prioritizing participation in urban planning over other pressing issues of everyday life is often practically, physically and mentally impossible. Their participation can only be sought when the process and goals accurately reflect the priorities and needs of those most socially and economically exposed. One possible way of addressing this can be the provision of childcare or economic or food-related compensation. But beyond being compensated for their time and effort, participants from socially unprivileged backgrounds must be reassured that their presence will bring about a material or qualitative improvement in their living conditions. In Amsterdam's ethnically diverse Indische Buurt neighborhood, the process of reading and commenting on financial documents for a participative budgeting scheme required residents to dedicate time and prior knowledge, effectively foreclosing the diversity of those who took part. The lack of guarantee that a proposal emerging from a position of socioeconomic vulnerability would be prioritized made the participation of "those in need" implausible. Indeed, the time they will need to invest to meaningfully engage with the process would be far larger than what they are able to afford, especially in comparison with individuals already equipped with such skills and knowledge.

Injustice also originates when "*the place from where*" participation takes place is not considered. There is a difference between those who speak on behalf of commercially interested groups, for example, and those who are there as residents. In the case of the Passeig de Sant Joan green avenue in Barcelona initiated in 2009, citizen participation processes ultimately involved more restaurant and business owners than local and immigrant families. The few neighborhood associations that do exist in the area ceded their participation to more economic-oriented groups. The dormant social texture in the local area represented by neighborhood associations with few members also played a role here, ceding their participation "space", or power, to groups who organize in defense of their economic returns. As a result, while the green corridor helped boost the appeal of the neighborhood as a green and revitalized area with increased public space and fancy eating venues, most Chinese-owned shops typical of the area disappeared. The overall tone of satisfaction expressed over the "clearing out" of Asian businesses to make way for more profitable tourist-friendly businesses, shared by the planning agency involved in the project, was an implicit indication of social discrimination. The limited citizen participation process also impacted the final design. While a neighborhood association located north of Passeig St. Joan advocated for a wide green pedestrian avenue, a "rambla" style, with small lanes for the cars on both ends, the city finally opted to expand sidewalks that allowed more space for bar and restaurant terraces (Kotsila et al. 2020).

Formality of representation is another formal barrier to the breadth of participation. The public engagement processes around the development of new green areas in Leipzig (Germany) show that it is often the individuals associated with a formal structure like an NGO that are more likely to partake in public consultations (Hörschelmann et al. 2017). In the case of Leipzig, public officials played a crucial role in enhancing meaningful inclusion, forging relationships with community organizations and residents and defending their interests at various levels of decision-making. Yet, participation formats that rest on formal organization membership for inclusion close the door on novel and alternative perspectives from the youth and marginalized groups, including migrants (Ibid.).

Finally, while civil participation is essential for urban sustainability transitions, we must address the patterns of exclusivity that exist even here and recognize the limits of volunteerism. In Western Europe, for example, many organic foods and renewable energy cooperatives tend to emerge from shared histories of place-based social–political mobilization, activism, cooperation and trust (Sekulova et al. 2017). But over-reliance on voluntary work for reaching urban sustainability targets can also result in the exploitation or exclusion of marginalized groups and reduce the long-term benefits of sustainability initiatives (Rosol 2012). A study of 63 grassroot sustainability initiatives from Finland, Germany, Italy, Romania, Scotland and Spain by scholars from the European research project TESS found them to be quite socioculturally homogenous: 84% of their users were country nationals, while a small fraction was non-European. In 54 of the studied initiatives, only 15% of their users were identified as low-income residents. Interviews further revealed that participants in community-based enterprises in the field of sustainability frequently failed to recognize their social privilege and the interests, needs and capacities of sociovulnerable groups (Argüelles et al. 2017). Indeed, some (urban) transition initiatives and activist collectives across Europe and North America have been facing important processes of critical self-reflection and even a crisis in representation over exclusionary practices and biases that must be addressed for justice to manifest at the level of grassroot sustainability practice (ECOLISE 2021).

Types of participatory processes

The kinds of issues around which participation takes place and how participation is enacted are two fundamental questions to consider in the context of urban environmental justice. Matters can vary from what some may consider trivial, such as which tree species to plant on a given street, to more substantial inquiries around large-scale urban remodeling. The first question can be illustrated by the issue of park maintenance in Newcastle, UK, where the municipal budget for sustaining the green infrastructure of the city was cut by over 90% as part of austerity measures implemented by the British government in 2016. That forced the city council to explore new funding opportunities. The proposed business plan envisioned the creation of new and diverse revenue streams mostly built on commercial activities in city parks and the engagement of citizens as volunteers for their maintenance. In turn, formal participative processes focused solely on refining the existing proposal for this new business model. Nevertheless, community groups advocated keeping parks as commons funded by public authorities. Concerns expressed by citizens with the creeping privatization and commercialization of the parks were disregarded as impertinent to the agenda of the consultations.

Second, how participation is orchestrated has a profound impact on the diversity of profiles and the depth of engagement of attendees, and consequently on justice. Participation events are frequently imbued with cultural codes which may be unfamiliar or alienating to certain ethnic minorities, or people with diverse educational and professional backgrounds (Cornwall 2008). Participative spaces need to be welcoming and tailored to the language, cultural, racial and gender specificities of a particular group. Self-exclusion due to the lack of self-confidence, trust or time is also a common factor that shapes participatory processes. While tailored focus groups tend to be inclusive, and enable in-depth participation, they may also face pressure to produce quick fixes or consensus, imbalanced group dynamics, issues of under-representativity or facilitation biases (Scott 2011). Performative action is another example of inclusive, in-depth participation that features a hands-on involvement approach to transforming city spaces, often in the context of community gardening in Western Europe. It is a materially grounded open-ended praxis that offers stakeholders the chance to design and act in each space. It is a particularly welcoming format for those who are not well-educated, nor speak the established languages in each territory, yet have a foot in, and access to, local performative spaces (Wilker et al. 2016). Nevertheless, in-depth participation measures like these must be coupled with broader methods including consultation and interviews to not produce skewed results.

Smart city digitization offers a spectrum of approaches toward participation, including phone apps or other online means of collecting opinions on proposed projects. Technological approaches to participation, however, provide an illusionary sense of inclusivity, especially in terms of allowing for deliberation between key actors. Two major issues are at hand there. First, digital participation is only accessible to those with technological literacy and access to the internet. Second, it can hardly be held accountable given that citizens cannot trace how data and opinions are processed and interpreted, especially if they are qualitative. Overall, there is little evidence that technology is improving the quality of participation (Wilker et al. 2016). In the city of Ghent, Belgium for example, despite having a department entirely devoted to citizen participation through both face-to-face processes and technology-based tools, reliance on digital participation was found to be ultimately exclusive for those who did not have access to or knowledge of digital platforms.

Importantly, participation processes are rarely smooth and unidirectional. They are necessarily spaces of contestation, where power relations are manifested and personal, collective, public and private priorities collide. When such antagonisms are not provided with the means to unfold, participation becomes limited, or tokenistic, and eventually conducive to entrenched power relations (White 1996). In this way, it is important that the cultural codes participatory processes may adhere to, such as courtesy and mildness of tone, do not smother critical concerns or illegitimate resistance. This is not to say that resistance is the single meaningful form of civic agency. In contexts of poverty, gender inequality and health deprivation, calls to resist all forms of power tend to immobilize (rather than empower) and can reflect or emanate from a rather privileged positionality (Kesby 2005).

Grassroots action and policy tools

A typical error when organizing participative processes is to think of them in isolation from decision-making. A central issue here is how and if participative processes inform policy. Even if a wide range of attendants have been attracted, and spaces for voicing multiple concerns have been created, justice is hardly ever guaranteed at the level of their fair interpretation and translation into political decisions. Maier et al. (2014) explored the way extensive civil participation in forest policy affects eventual decision-making and its overall framing. The authors found that the efforts to raise participation standards in forest policy are hardly influencing the ideological framing and interests of the public institutions. There was little policy learning among the representatives of public institutions, and little improvement in the relation between those representing the business sector and the ones involved in conservation. While this example comes from peri-urban areas, it speaks to the urban domain, where subtle forms of grants-based coercion can be used to generate consent across the civil society around the need to use market-based instruments to enhance urban forestry, even if these privileges are mostly white, well-off neighborhoods (Perkins 2011).

Achieving systemic and regular citizen participation in urban planning partly resides in establishing trust, which is slow to build and quick to dissolve. Citizens must be able to trace the way their inputs, voices and concerns are considered, or not, in making policy decisions, especially considering socioeconomic, ethnic, racial and cultural differences, and disempowerment associated with social marginalization. In other words, the limited translation of participation processes into public decisions and policies tends to leave a deeper scar on those who are more socially vulnerable or economically precarious. Participation processes involving vulnerable groups should only take place if the organizers are committed to making a thorough and nuanced reading of the results.

Changing the formats, breadth and depth of citizen participation in urban planning is not an easy task. It requires a massive shift in perceptions, attitudes and relations with and within public institutions and dominant economic players. Unlocking the transformational potential of citizen participation requires spaces where different perspectives and disagreements can unfold. This is particularly important in considering the priorities and needs of those who are socially and economically vulnerable or marginalized. If institutional formats feature more process-oriented methods and downscale expectations around reaching immediate, reasonable and rational results, the citizen participation spaces can be a little more inclusive for a diversity of participants. A fundamental way to challenge and transform the currently limited citizen participation in urban planning is through widening its thematic range, and allowing for strategic questions, such as models of city governance, or the existing urbanization paradigms, to be unpacked and continuously (re)discussed or (re)evaluated. While such efforts may be exhausting, they produce, reproduce and continuously nourish a culture of participation that is essential to addressing many of the drivers of injustice discussed throughout this book.

Selective civic participation and inclusion in greening in Nantes

Crossed by two rivers, the Loire and L'Erdre, Nantes is a dynamic postindustrial city that successfully converted large shipyard areas into new centers of biotechnology and art, public transit and cycling lanes, and blue and green areas. As a result, the 300,000 residents living in Nantes have access to 57 m² of green space per capita and more than 100 municipal parks and gardens. Through a yearly investment of close to 30 million euros, renaturing projects have also been vertically integrated into an economic model that brings together gardeners, urban farmers, landscape architects, horticulture and permaculture specialists scattered across the 1,000 family gardens in the city.

Nantes' emblematic sustainable regeneration includes the conversion of the Ile de Nantes into a mixed residential, design and information technology district bordered by new parks and waterfront areas, and the creation of eco-districts such as Bottière Chenaie. In many ways, Nantes is committed to co-designing, co-producing and co-managing many of the green spaces, gardens and greenways it has created or sponsored with residents. Several years in a row, families have been encouraged to bring artistic creations to exhibitions in the Jardin des Plantes. Others have practiced gardening in the 14 organic family gardens next to Parc des Oblates.

However, the municipality has received criticism from civic groups for encouraging participatory activities only once it has decided upon the use of space, while invisibilizing or discouraging more informal and less manicured green spaces and activities. Many feel that the municipality only works with the groups and networks with which it has historic relations or political affiliations, or with the city administration. Residents also critique the municipality for failing to integrate the working-class and racialized residents of what are called "priority safety zones" such as Bellevue and Malakov. Several civic groups from the Projets Contestés mapping project feel that well-being, livability and quality of life for all are no longer at the center of the city's agenda, which rather prioritizes the "metropolization" of Nantes in order to attract highly qualified residents as part of the new economy.

Rather than remaining a smaller-scale, welcoming city where all residents have a say in the future trajectory of the city, Nantes aims to attract visitors and newcomers that can stimulate its economy and boost its image as a sustainable green city. In a move that many consider an act of greenwashing or "museification of the green", Nantes invested a huge budget in artistic green projects like the Jardin Extraordinaire et its associated l'Arbre aux Hérons, designed by famous local artists François Delaroziere and Pierre Orefice, to materialize their vision of the city. The Arbre au Hérons is a 52 million euro mechanical tree with suspended gardens linked to the well-known Les Machines de l'Île cultural site on the Ile de Nantes. It is meant to be a space that residents and tourists can enjoy as visitors to an artistic exhibit.

Other redevelopment projects are criticized for their top-down nature. Currently under construction, the Doulon-Gohards large-scale ZAC redevelopment project next to the Vieux-Doulon neighborhood in Eastern Nantes will contain 2,700 housing units and four urban farms that threaten 180 ha of former agricultural land, including a semi-natural 1.5 ha space built and used by residents and the civic group Jardin des Ronces. Although the ZAC scheme mandates the construction of more than 50% of units as public and social housing, residents disagree with the scale of the project and the lack of protection of peri-urban land. In their view, the city is hypocritical for projecting an image of environmental sustainability and land preservation while erasing the rural–urban border and natural spaces on the edge of the city to attract high-end residents eager to live close to urban farms. These critiques consider that the scale of the project and the urban encroachment demonstrate a lack of consideration of alternative uses proposed by residents and a disrespect for urban peripheries (Baró and Anguelovski 2021).

Note

1 Global Platform for the Right to the City: www.right2city.org/the-right-to-the-city/.

Figure 9 Power-Knowledge Asymmetries

9   Driver 9

Power-knowledge asymmetries

Urban sustainability is a field of theory and practice where different sciences, disciplines and kinds of expertise meet the lived realities and struggles of citizens, actions of practitioners and role of local governments in cities. When referring to knowledge around urban sustainability, we thus refer to the formal, technical and scientific insight, as well as the knowledge generated through hands-on experience of and with communities. As sustainability becomes a core policy and political field in cities around the world (Wilson 2015), what counts as valid knowledge for sustainability can reflect and reproduce patterns of power imbalance in society (Foucault 1980). Struggles in the terrain of knowledge can take place in less spectacular ways, be more nuanced and subtle, and unfold over long periods of time. While socioenvironmental conflicts over access to things like housing, green space, clean environments and healthcare often take center stage in discussions relating to sustainability in cities, struggles over knowledge are essentially power struggles, and thus especially relevant for social and environmental justice (Figure 9).

Unequal access to sustainability and its benefits is not only about physical accessibility but also about access to knowledge and information concerning the decision-making processes around the design, implementation and assessment of sustainability interventions. In this regard, inequality may manifest in the knowledge hierarchies of governmental or academic institutions, between institutions (municipalities, governments and universities) and more informal associations, or among social groups at the local level. It is often the case, for example, that local groups trying to implement sustainability projects such as community gardens or food-sharing initiatives lack knowledge on technical aspects, legal regulations or available support schemes that could enable them to realize their ideas (Kotsila et al. 2020).

Struggles over knowledge also implicate what kind of knowledge is recognized as valid when negotiating or imagining urban sustainability. This

DOI: 10.4324/9781003221425-10

can be expressed, for example, in how sustainability is defined or assessed by different scientific disciplines (economics, ecology and social sciences) and by extension, different governmental departments or non-governmental organizations. Consequently, the questions asked and tools used to study sustainability will define the knowledge generated around it. A core challenge for organizations such as municipalities is to facilitate meaningful communication across departments in balancing their priorities toward sustainability policies (e.g., between urban ecology, land use, housing and economy) when these often contradict.

How non-scientific knowledge is accounted for in urban sustainability planning is also central to the analyses of representational and recognitional justice. A justice approach to urban sustainability would require the inclusion of local, embodied, experiential and traditional knowledge, especially those of historically marginalized and vulnerable communities, regarding the benefits or shortcomings of certain forms of sustainability over others (see Chapter 8). Dominant techno-scientific and managerial approaches to sustainability have been criticized for depoliticizing and deepening inequalities (Cook and Swyngedouw 2012), given that they are stripped of the conflictual essence inherent to any type of socioenvironmental change (see Chapter 6). The assumption that conflicting interests in society can be automatically resolved through sustainability interventions can render the claims and demands of underprivileged groups invisible.

In this chapter, we examine how inequalities and imbalances in knowledge structures around sustainability act as a driver of injustice along two key themes: knowledge hierarchies and clashing epistemologies; and the pitfalls of knowledge translation, exchange and communication around sustainability. We then turn to briefly describe how attention to the everyday, embodied and situated knowledge can allow for more justice-attuned analyses of socioenvironmental change and knowledge generation around sustainability.

Knowledge hierarchies and clashing epistemologies around sustainability

What types of knowledge count as valid when identifying sustainability challenges or solutions? Power-knowledge asymmetries are reflected both in terms of who and in what context sustainability claims are made. In the case of powerful groups and institutions, both produce knowledge that dominates and dominate through knowledge that becomes regarded as most valid in society (Foucault 1980). Meanwhile, the knowledge of marginalized communities, which usually takes the form of experiential accounts and embodied perceptions, is rendered non-scientific, too specific, too irrational or too political, and is thus disregarded or discarded as not valid. Through their project on "toxic bios",[1] Armiero et al. (2019) underline this epistemic or narrative injustice through cases of environmental contamination. They reveal how stories of toxicity and contamination provided by people whose embodied experiences of risk exposure are questioned and discarded are in fact stories "about the construction and legitimation of knowledge" (Ibid.). This has also been the case with new, supposedly sustainable urban interventions. In Medellin, Colombia, a top-down initiative to set up an urban agriculture project in low-income neighborhoods entirely disregarded the knowledge and historical relationships of locals with the land—key for preserving traditions and securing livelihoods—dispossessing them of access to nature, land, social capital and voice (Anguelovski, Irazábal-Zurita, and Connolly 2019b). In contrast, in Dublin, Ireland, local officials considered the vernacular knowledge of communities concerning the quality of their local environments, resulting in the Bridgefoot Street project currently under construction in the working-class neighborhood of The Liberties. The plot of land, once reserved for new real estate development, was eventually equipped with a park, thanks to the demands made by residents for more public and safe green spaces in a historically gray neighborhood with high levels of youth disengagement. Their claims garnered support from the urban ecology department, enabling the plot to be classified as green space (Kotsila et al. 2020).

With these examples in mind, it is important to consider the notion of epistemic justice when discussing the role of power-knowledge asymmetries as a potential driver of injustice in urban sustainability. Fricker (2007) defines epistemic injustice as a kind of wrong done to a person or a group, specifically regarding their capacity as a knower. In this sense, she distinguishes two forms of epistemic injustice: *testimonial* and *hermeneutical*. Testimonial injustice occurs when prejudice shadows the testimonies of marginalized and discriminated groups, making their narratives, accounts and views less credible. An example of testimonial injustice is evident in the case of Tolka Valley Park in Dublin, Ireland, where long-stigmatized traveler communities were not recognized with the right to continue using the park to graze their horses, despite being part of a cultural practice protected by law. New barriers and walls were installed to reassure the more affluent communities living in new apartments southwest of the park that "criminal activity" would be controlled. While demands for a football pitch or physical barriers between the two communities were listened to and considered, horse-grazing practices were outright branded as criminal, adding to a long history of discrimination against travelers (Kiss, Sekulova, and Kotsila 2019). Hermeneutical injustice, on the other hand, takes place when experiences of harm are not recognized as such in each process, community or in society more broadly. In urban greening, for example, it has been documented that the creation or regeneration of new green amenities like parks or riverfronts has often excluded or disregarded the experiences and practices of racialized and marginalized groups (Finney 2014). When such long-term knowledge and memory held by communities of color around violence associated with specific types of natural landscapes are disregarded in processes of urban planning, trauma is reproduced and ultimately alienates these groups from new sustainable and health-promoting environments in a form of hermeneutical and distributive injustice (Ranganathan and Bratman 2021; Anguelovski et al. 2020).

Questions of knowledge and power, and their repercussions on justice, also pertain to how dominant discourses around sustainability are created. Whose ideologies, cultures, visions and imaginations are reproduced in dominant performances and forms of sustainability? In order to develop thinking on just sustainabilities, Castán-Broto and Westman (2019) define as key, "the possibility to decolonize sustainability knowledge and the opportunity to bring to the fore a wide diversity of values and understandings of urban sustainability . . . to understand how sustainability has become an inherent part of structures of oppression" (Ibid.). Attention to local, embodied and situated knowledge is central to decentering knowledge on urban sustainability and avoiding blueprint solutions that not only ignore local context but also write out existing alternative visions and practices of what sustainability and justice might look like. In cities like New Delhi, Cape Town and Barcelona, informal waste picking/skarreling is a practice that provides some form of livelihood to poor people and contributes to material reuse with almost zero side-losses in energy or materials. Yet it is far from being considered a sustainability action and is rather socially stigmatized and unrecognized by formal institutions (de Barcegol and Gowda 2020; van Heerden 2015).

Engaging with informality can expand and decenter the gaze of sustainability beyond the mainstream paradigm and single horizon of the "Western global city". This has direct justice implications for places and people that have followed different patterns of urbanization had different cultures of inhabiting urban spaces and performed a different kind of sustainability (Robinson 2005). Ananya Roy (2011) applies this lens by taking a closer look at informal, self-built settlements found in many urban and suburban areas situated mainly, but not exclusively, in the Global South. Often pejoratively labeled as slums, Roy instead describes them as "terrains of habitation, livelihood, self-organization and politics", contradicting typical narratives that portray these areas and their inhabitants as illegal, risk-prone and unwanted. Recognizing subaltern spaces and people as transformative agents in urban life challenges dominant Western assumptions about sustainability ontologically, epistemologically and empirically. In Europe, too, minorities and other marginalized groups like immigrants from poorer countries are often not regarded as environmental citizens, and rather in need of being socialized into sustainability. Research with Somali immigrants in Manchester, UK, however, showed that significant knowledge and practices relating to household sustainability (e.g., growing food at home, following diets low in animal products and recycling) do travel from non-Western to Western contexts, with religion and care practices being strong motivators for continuing to engage in such practices (MacGregor, Walker, and Katz-Gerro 2019).

Pitfalls of knowledge translation, exchange and communication

Exclusivity of access in relation to urban sustainability and its benefits can also be the result of difficult terminology, unwelcoming communication platforms, failure to translate insights into useful resources for practitioners or citizens, and the lack of participatory processes in decision-making. In Berlin, Germany, an initiative to set up public refrigerators to share food and reduce waste was faced with the challenge of navigating official regulations around food safety and hygiene and differing views about how to best manage such initiatives (Morrow 2019). This example demonstrates how decisions around safety and risk build on power-knowledge dynamics and are often left to experts, especially when they concern systems bound with complexity such as food or sustainability.

Pluralizing spaces for negotiating or redefining sustainability toward more just horizons would require both the popularization of scientific knowledge and the incorporation of situated knowledge and local perceptions into sustainability policy and action. Effective, inclusive and socially considerate knowledge brokerage can enhance the justice aspect of urban sustainability interventions, especially when it includes and brings benefits to underprivileged and vulnerable groups (Partidario and Sheate 2013; van der Velden 2004). By knowledge brokerage, we refer to the processes that include facilitating knowledge exchange or sharing between researchers, practitioners and policymakers. Co-creation, for example, is an approach implemented in cities with the objective to facilitate the circulation of ideas, understandings and cutting-edge research among a diverse variety of actors in society. Trencher et al. (2013) explore this notion of knowledge co-creation in the "triple-academic actors engaging with government, industry and civil society" toward the design and implementation of sustainability interventions that are more informed, better contextualized and with a higher chance of being transformative. Examples of this include "living labs", "city labs" or "experimentation labs", as new and unconventional modes of participation in urban spaces and as part of multiple stakeholder partnerships, knowledge brokerage and co-learning. However, these have also faced criticism for the extent to which they may reproduce injustice, especially when knowledge about complex issues of sustainability is shared and asserted mainly between high-level bureaucrats, academics and policymakers, excluding more grassroots demands, experiences and knowledge.

While the goal of knowledge brokerage and co-creation is to better understand and address urban challenges and socioenvironmental injustices by breaking institutional and disciplinary silos, the same processes can reproduce patterns of exclusion like what is observed in citizen participation (see also Chapter 8). When these processes do not invite and facilitate the direct, meaningful and long-term participation of activists, local community groups, marginalized groups and minorities, they can lead to the erasure or misrepresentation of the values, views, interests and claims coming "from below", and thus fail to confront deeper systemic and structural inequalities at play. In the context of placemaking in US cities with respect to indigenous groups, Barry and Agyeman (2020) stress how it is "entirely insufficient if not dangerous" to assume that by inserting indigenous art in the urban landscape to enhance placemaking in relation to indigeneity in US cities, urban planning in any way addresses the historical erasure of indigenous culture in urbanism. They instead propose the creation of spaces and places that would allow for indigenous knowledge, practices and kinship relations to (re-)emerge. Similarly, knowledge brokerage, exchange and co-creation for urban sustainability and justice can only be conceptualized based on a deeper engagement with communities that are commonly left outside the walls or imaginations of urban planning.

The field of sustainability can be exclusive simply due to the inaccessibility of information around sustainable initiatives, whether in terms of language, format or availability. This can become a driver of injustice by limiting the potential for participation, stewardship or uptake of sustainability. For example, urban planning interventions such as cycle lanes, park creation or the transformation of unused land or buildings that welcome citizen participation through digital means may exclude less tech-literate populations such as the elderly or those with no reliable internet connection. In Ljubljana, small-scale farmers had little awareness of production networks that they could join and benefit from, and scant knowledge of best practices to reach a broader range of consumers. This lack of access to information was hampering the farmers' ability to compete against larger industrialized agricultural businesses and limiting the availability of locally sourced fresh food for urban consumers (Wascher et al. 2015).

Grassroots action and policy tools

Many critical environmental justice scholars have noted how planning for sustainable and just cities could benefit from the "small data", that is, the empirical accounts and relational stories of people whose health and well-being have been at stake considering environmental change (Privitera, Armiero, and Gravagno 2021). "Street science" is the term Corburn (2005) gave to the concerns of lay publics, especially low-income populations and people of color who have historically been most vulnerable to environmental and climate health risks. Studying racially and ethnically diverse communities in Greenpoint/Williamsburg in Brooklyn, New York, he shows how their knowledge of environmental risks can democratize the study and decision-making process around issues such as water and air pollution, also providing low-cost policy solutions and adding to the knowledge base of policy (Ibid.). Alongside incorporating such vernacular or lay knowledge, in an approach often referred to also as citizen science (Funtowicz and Ravetz 1993), just urban planning for sustainability also requires a knowledge perspective that is feminist and intersectional. In other words, it must be informed by the long-term knowledge of disenfranchised, racialized and otherwise marginalized communities and consider the different positionalities and subjectivities within and across such communities (Amorim-Maia et al. 2022; Doshi 2017).

A key contribution of feminist thinking is the notion that knowledge is necessarily partial, contextualized, situated and embodied. In this regard, a focus on everyday practices and behaviors can deepen analyses of injustice by illuminating the embodied and situated knowledge of people in relation to local environments, resource use, waste and toxicity. These are all deeply relevant to sustainability. For example, as Truelove (2011) describes, access to water for residents of urban informal settlements in India not only is a matter of quantity and quality in rich versus poor neighborhoods, but involves intimate, meaningful and power-laden embodiments, mostly experienced by the women in charge of securing safe water for their households (Ibid.). These are important lessons to understand, for example, why certain development schemes for water and sanitation via micro-credit in poor communities will not achieve the desired sustainability and health impacts in an equitable way if they don't engage with local understandings and practices around hygiene, every day and gendered realities of water use, and traditional health knowledges (Kotsila and Saravanan 2017).

Rendering multiple forms, perspectives and sources of knowledge as both valid and valuable, however, Donna Haraway (1988) warns, should not fall into the trap of relativizing everything. Where one "sees from", in terms of knowledge production, is a political act. Taking the vantage point of the subjugated stands better chances of producing "worlds less organized by axes of domination", but nonetheless is not unproblematic; a reality that highlights how subjugated knowledges should therefore also be subject to "critical reexamination, decoding, deconstruction and interpretation" (Ibid.: 584). Thinking through embodied urban political ecology can provide a better understanding of often-contradictory desires and behaviors of oppressed groups as they navigate resistance/docility and contestation/co-optation. In the example of Mumbai, as Doshi (2017) describes, some women supported the elite redevelopment of the slums they used to inhabit, in hopes of better living conditions through resettlement, while others were opposed to and fought against such displacement and discrimination.

Prioritizing technical knowledge to address climate resilience in East Boston

The 2017 Climate Ready Plan for East Boston (City of Boston n.d.), a historically working-class Latinx and Italian neighborhood next to the city of Boston's airport, forecasted that 50% of the land could be flooded by a major storm event in the next 50 years. As part of this plan and other related initiatives, East Boston has since received funding to create new green resilient projects or upgrade existing green infrastructure, such as Piers Park and the East Boston Greenway. The neighborhood is also part of the large-scale 2018 Resilient Boston Harbor plan, with goals of creating green infrastructure projects such as elevated green landscapes and resilient parks along the 47 miles of Boston's shoreline. Interestingly, part of the Harbor Plan has been designed as inclusive and participatory, involving community-centered planning to address lower-income and racialized residents' needs and priorities.

In order to give birth to those plans and projects, the city of Boston hired the engineering consultancy firm *Kleinfelder* in 2016–2017 to develop resiliency engineering and regulatory and policy recommendations for coastal infrastructure to protect vulnerable areas of East Boston (and neighboring Charlestown) against sea level rise and storm surge flooding. It also worked to "generate political buy-in through extensive stakeholder engagement" (Kleinfelder n.d.). From *Kleinfelder*'s perspective, the workshops, and meetings that its staff organized, were inclusionary and participatory. Among others, the firm representatives met with local environmental justice and housing groups to identify the type of infrastructure projects that could address resilience needs. This infrastructure included "elevated parks, multi-purpose berms, and nature-based barriers" as ways of increasing security in the face of climate events, creating new waterfront access and increasing mobility (Ibid.).

While *Kleinfelder* was aware of broader affordability issues in this gentrifying neighborhood, especially so for rental families, the staff identified such concerns as outside their domain of intervention and as a prerogative and responsibility of the municipality. Their priority was to gather data on technical issues and conduct their work in a fast-paced, six-month time frame through community open houses and meetings with groups inside and outside the municipality. According to them, their aim was to target data reporting on environmental and technical aspects or "physical components" rather than associated socioeconomic and sociocultural ones.

For many residents, *Kleinfelder* represented a wealthy out-of-town New York firm coming into their neighborhood uninvited and imposing their timelines, logistics and expertise on residents, and engaging in a superficial form of engagement that is later disregarded in the projects proposed by external consultants. According to a longtime environmental activist in the area:

> "They [firm representatives] come in with their own [predetermined] ideas. You can't just walk into a neighborhood where you're not welcome and simply ask residents what they need".

One specific concern voiced by residents was that external consultants came in with a fixed idea on which residents were made to vote, pushing them to prioritize climate solutions presented by the firm. Residents also regretted that this consultancy work ignored past community-based research experiences led by local environmental groups, which had revealed that what "community residents in this lower-income family neighborhood really want is active parks, active open spaces" rather than passive typologies of green infrastructure.

The municipality-sponsored consultancy work also seems to have disregarded an academic needs assessment document led by a group of community-involved researchers who worked across groups and classes. According to that same activist, it "was academic research with valid results, which they completely ignored". This research included the identification of economic needs, especially those related to the protection of small businesses and retail against gentrification and displacement, and their connection to broader resilience issues. It also identified the need for community connection to green infrastructure projects. This finding contrasts with the city-sponsored consultancy, which mostly left aside gentrification concerns as expressed by residents as well as their sociocultural needs to take greater ownership of green infrastructure projects. Here, knowledge was gathered in a restrictive manner and included only partial, very specific data previously prioritized by both consultants and the city.

Note

1 www.toxicbios.eu/#/stories

Figure 10 The Growth Imperative and Neoliberal Urbanism

10 Driver 10

The growth imperative and neoliberal urbanism

Economic growth, a fundamental element of capitalist development, has long been fetishized (Schmelzer 2015) and used as *the* baseline measure of societal progress and development (Escobar 1995). Predicated upon patriarchal, racial and military domination (Mies 2014; Salleh 2009), the pursuit of economic growth drives many of the socioecological injustices and climatic changes occurring in cities and beyond. The trickle-down argument, or rather illusion, born from the notion that only by making the economic pie bigger, can we grow the slice of those at the bottom, has continuously failed (Hickel 2017). Unpaid labor (Mies 2014) and finite biophysical resources largely sustain economic growth, leading Herman Daly to suggest that growth had become "uneconomic" since the 1970s (Daly 1996). Growth-driven injustices in the urban sphere and beyond continue to expand, despite the recent focus of sustainability discourse and action on the "green growth" or "smart growth" paradigm (Figure 10).

The increasing monetary value of all goods and services produced in a country, known as the gross domestic product (GDP), is the common, internationally dominant, denominator measuring the success of most public policies, including urban sustainability planning (Krähmer 2021). The use of GDP as an indicator of progress has been severely criticized, mostly for failing to factor in environmental devastation, natural resource depletion and household and unpaid work, or what some authors call "the core economy" (Mies 2014). In addition, the implications of the growth imperative for urban social justice are multiple. These can be the first cast in terms of economic precarity and livelihoods' vulnerability (see Chapter 1). Continuous economic growth requires economies of scale through increased efficiency, productivity gains, financialization and speculation. Crucially, however, economic growth is premised upon the availability and continuous reproduction of a cheap, often feminized, and racialized, precarious labor force within and across national borders, held in weak bargaining position vis-à-vis employers (Salleh 2009). Even if economic growth has

DOI: 10.4324/9781003221425-11

been associated with drastic rises in living standards for millions of people in the Global North over the last 200 years, the gap between the haves and have-nots has widened, especially across class, race and gender (Pickett and Wilkinson 2010). The rising social disparity and psychological distress worldwide associated with economic growth—and the related elite capture of growth-driven revenues—is well articulated in cities, where racialized, working-class populations are frequently relegated to poor housing and public service provision, reduced access to affordable quality food and limited sustainability amenities.

While there were efforts from the state in mid-twentieth-century North America and Europe to redistribute the benefits of growth and provide social goods and services, the rise of neoliberalism in the 1970s saw its steady, albeit uneven, withdrawal as the market took precedence. In the urban sphere, entrepreneurial forms of urbanism and urban governance focused on new ways of fostering local economic development and employment growth while generating inter-urban competition. Neoliberal urbanization refers to urban transformations embedded within neoliberalization processes, including, for example, the deregulation of urban land, the rolling back of state intervention in planning and the growing reliance on privatization in light of diminishing state support for welfare and local services (Swyngedouw et al. 2002). Furthermore, neoliberal urbanization both exploits and produces sociospatial differences.

When the logic of neoliberal urbanism permeates urban sustainability initiatives, economic development and growth are prioritized over environmental benefits, which are either regarded as a bonus or instrumentalized in various forms of "greenwashing", while justice and other social dimensions are absent. A range of critical terms is used to articulate the inner workings of neoliberal urbanism in relation to (un)sustainability, including the neoliberalization of (urban) nature (Kotsila, Anguelovski et al. 2021), the enclosure of (urban) commons and planetary urbanization. We explore these concepts in more depth, focusing on their implications for urban (in)justice and the ability to counteract them to generate more equitable and green urban environments.

Neoliberalization of urban nature and commons enclosure

In recent decades, cities are increasingly expected to drive the growth of global economies even though urbanization is a major driver of climate change and intensifying climate change impacts. The green, resilient, smart and sustainable city ultimately seeks win–win solutions for both environmentalism and economic growth in liberal economies (Anguelovski and

Alier 2014), which is increasingly pursued through neoliberal tactics and processes. Either the state withdraws from the provision of goods and services (through privatizations, deregulations) and takes a managerial role that focuses on profit rather than equity (Perkins 2011) or restructures itself adopting neoliberal logic within its modes of governance and regulatory relations (Peck and Tickell 2002).

The neoliberalization of nature takes place not only through the direct capture and commodification of natural resources such as water or land but also through the capturing of pro-environmental discourse (McCarthy and Prudham 2004). In the context of increasing global environmental pressures largely fueled by the continued pursuit of economic growth (Keyßer and Lenzen 2021), most attempts at defending the growth rhetoric are characterized by a use of appealing descriptors such as "green", "inclusive" or "smart" (Hickel and Kallis 2020). In this respect, urban sustainability discourses often end up turning what started out as radical ideas for intervention into system-affirming tools that do not question the growth imperative (Sekulova et al. 2017; Tulloch and Neilson 2014).

Urban nature and urban interventions that aim to address environmental and climate change are governed in an increasingly neoliberal fashion that features fuzzy concepts and "ivy discourses" such as nature-based solutions (Kotsila, Anguelovski et al. 2021), sustainability (Swyngedouw 2007) or transformation (Westman and Castán Broto 2022). Green buildings, for example, have been portrayed as the epitome of sustainability in cities through aesthetics that provide a false impression of sustainability (Sekulova et al. 2021). A good example of this is the Vertical Forest (Bosco Verticale) in Milan, Italy, comprising two skyscrapers containing 24 and 17 floors each that house 800 trees, 4,500 bushes and 15,000 plants (Di Paola 2021). Despite its sustainability claims, clearly the significant amount of material extraction and transport involved in the building's construction and its use of concrete cannot be offset by the vegetation adorning its façade. Not only are the apartments far beyond the reach of most working Italians—selling for a whopping seven million euros—the skyscrapers are one of several luxury complexes driving up rents and displacing long-term residents in the area. This exemplifies how "sustainability-fixes" (While et al. 2004) and urban boosterism agendas (García-Lamarca et al. 2021) do not address the pervasive need for economic growth at the cost of social exclusion and global environmental deterioration.

The financialization of greening is another manifestation of the neoliberalization of nature, whereby smart techno-financial innovation is building new relationships between nature and society based on return-on-investment logic. Green finance is often unproblematically imagined as a way to build sustainable (urban) futures, with no reflection on what this means in practice (Bigger and Millington 2020). Fitting hand in glove with "roll-out" neoliberalism rationality (Peck and Tickell 2002), the deployment of financial instruments such as green bonds in Gothenburg appeared to generate win–win situations—feel good through buying green bonds because you are contributing to a sustainable world, plus get a stable and positive return on your investment—but in practice, the investment of bond funding does not change the broader unequal and unjust urban environment (García-Lamarca and Ullström 2022).

Processes of nature neoliberalization are also taking place through the enclosure of the commons. This process is aimed at finding new outlets for capital accumulation by controlling the use and exchange value of urban space or shutting down access to any urban space or sociality that creates non-commodified means of reproduction (Hodkinson 2012). Commons enclosure is a historic process illustrated today by the privatization or commodification of green and public space use. A new park called the Library of Trees, situated between the Vertical Forest skyscrapers in Milan, constitutes an elite and increasingly privatized green space whose management was entrusted to the private developer Manfredi Catella to save maintenance costs. In exchange, the municipality allowed Catella to organize events and place commercial amenities on the site (Di Paola 2021). In places like Dublin, green spaces built by developers with the condition that they would remain open to the public have been gated, such as those of The Mills student housing in The Liberties (Anguelovski et al. 2021b). In Barcelona, this dynamic is increasingly illustrated by the demolition of informal community gardens like Hort de la Vanguardia in the Poblenou district, to make way for the front lawns of high-end hotels.

Planetary urbanization

The planetary urbanization concept is a critical justice-related implication of the growth imperative associated with the relentless production and transformation of sociospatial organization across scales and territories (Brenner 2018). Based on the sociologist and urban philosopher Henri Lefebvre's (2003) view that the world is becoming increasingly urbanized, the term refers to the expansion of urban territories and lifestyles across virtually every corner of the globe, creating landscapes of sociospatial difference (Arboleda 2016). Economic growth and capital accumulation, largely entrenched in the notion of "development" (Escobar 1995), are the major factors that underpin the scale and speed of planetary urbanization. The high metabolic cost of (sub)urban middle-class lifestyles, also known as the imperial mode of living (Brand and Wissen 2021), is grounded in the unlimited appropriation of resources, disproportionate claims to global and local ecosystems and cheap labor from "elsewhere". The costs of producing and transporting the key commodities required for an urban "imperial mode of living", though largely invisible in urban space, follow a logic of neoliberal urbanization in terms of a continuous extension of commodification and market rule.

Planetary urbanization also highlights the uneven distribution of wealth and the reliance of urban expansion on remote material and resource extraction in ways that shift the environmental and socioeconomic costs onto territories and bodies in the peri-urban space or further away, forcing displacement, conflict and migration (Conde et al. 2022). The same holds true with sustainability innovations around the "smart" or "service city" and their high cost in terms of disrupted livelihoods and communities. As a result, rapid urbanization is the driving factor of capital accumulation because of the raw and transformed material resources it mobilizes from around the globe from forests, mines, rivers and their related road, port and airport infrastructures (Brenner 2018), which in turn produce inequalities and conflicts in the extracted territories and communities.

The costs of urban regeneration, expansion and growth-driven sustainability measures are therefore shed not only in terms of excluding vulnerable or disenfranchised communities at the level of the city but manifested along the international production chains in the form of dispossession, exploitation, contamination, criminalization, impoverishment and violence elsewhere. Urban environmental justice cannot thus be conceived in isolation from global extractivist pressures or global environmental justice struggles. Analyzing 2,743 cases of environmental conflicts across the globe, Scheidel et al. (2020) find that environmental defenders, and indigenous activists in particular, face very high rates of criminalization, physical violence and assassinations worldwide. Henceforth, addressing urban environmental injustice in the context of European or North American cities requires addressing "cost shifting" practices that create or fuel ecological conflicts and engaging with the disproportionate socioecological debt owed to the South by the North (Warlenius et al. 2015).

Planetary urbanization and urban growth are also sustained by the increasing role of global finance, including real estate developers, investors, equity firms and pension funds in local economies (Soederberg and Walks 2017) and their increasing returns in extracting land and development value. Their ability to shape the urban environment is facilitated by neoliberal governance rules and arrangements, including market-driven deregulation and re-regulation, privatization of public land, new zoning laws and easy permitting mechanisms; defunding and sale of social and public housing, asset-based social policies and managerial approaches in public administrations. As a result, global cities like Vancouver, Boston, London or Dublin are hosting thousands of new, empty luxury buildings owned by equity funds and global landlords waiting for land value and profits to accrue. In London in 2018, 6,100 ultra-high net worth individuals—people with assets, not including property, of £20 million or more—had second homes in the city. One in 20 homes are empty in Central and West London, as are half of the residences in new buildings, and as are 19% of units across the city's inner boroughs (Atkinson 2018). In a time of austerity politics, municipal governments find it much more lucrative to support the private sector rather than finance or maintain high stocks of social housing.

Whether through safeguarding financialization or investment in road infrastructure, real estate development or large and mostly unused projects, growth and urban expansion are seen as the single policy means to fight unemployment and social inequality. It is advocated by those who promote austerity as well as those who support expansionary Keynesian policies (Sekulova et al. 2017). The results of both growth strategies are, however, identical. Social and environmental burdens are shifted across territories, bodies and generations, while environmental injustice and ecological crises amass and grow.

Grassroots action and policy tools

The hypothesis that a democratically led, redistributive and equitable downsizing of the global economy and change of economic paradigm could not only sustain but also improve human well-being, social justice and environmental sustainability has underpinned much of the academic research on degrowth over the past ten years (Demaria et al. 2013). Understandings of degrowth take various forms, from an umbrella vision for radical change to a multidisciplinary academic paradigm to a movement that advocates a shift from the growth ideology and the coloniality of power and modernity (Abazeri 2022). Several degrowth policy proposals are especially relevant to urban environmental justice and sustainability. The introduction of a universal basic income at municipal, regional or national levels could reduce the social stigma associated with unemployment benefits while enhancing peoples' capacity to overturn exploitative and precarious labor relations. Financing could be achieved by modest increases in the taxes paid by the richest 15% of the population (Paulson et al. 2020). Universal care income is a related proposal that highlights the social recognition of unpaid and highly gendered care work performed to sustain life and well-being at the level of households and communities (Ibid.). Finally, reducing weekly working hours could increase employment, while liberating individuals from the excessive labor obligations in their lifetime (Kallis et al. 2013).

Mobilizations that prefigure degrowth outside and in the peripheries of public institutions abound and proliferate. (Re)commoning practices, for example, around the municipalization of water, renewable sources of energy, cooperative housing or communal management of land ensure the accessibility of basic services across vulnerable groups. Acts of commoning, understood as self-provisioning governance systems and a set of social solidarity and care practices that exist outside the market and the state, have provided a powerful response to individualistic solutionism in the frame of neoliberalism (Stavrides 2020). The rise of bottom-up initiatives in the field of urban sustainability—including community gardens, local food, housing, energy and transport cooperatives, along with the multiple movements resisting gentrification, "touristic monocultures" (like Barcelona's Neighborhood Assembly for Tourism Degrowth), high-speed transport infrastructure and other socioenvironmental pressures—jointly prefigure degrowth futures.

Luxury developments and empty buildings in green and smart growth Vancouver

Vancouver is regularly prized as one of the world's most livable and green cities. Back in 2012, the city sets a goal for itself to become the world's greenest city by 2020 and was later ranked in 2014 by the Global Green Economy Index as the fourth greenest city in the world. The Vancouver green model brings together open and green space development, green energy, sustainable transit and building densification through taller, vertical construction and a reduction of urban sprawl. This model has been largely supported by what is known as the EcoDensity Initiative, officially launched in 2006 to combine livability, affordability and environmental sustainability. It does so, however, without questioning the "hegemony" of "smart growth" (Rosol 2013). As a result, this type of green branding has largely translated into global real estate speculation, large-scale real estate development and prohibitive housing costs.

Over the last two decades, EcoDensity has given much priority to sustainable transit, with an emphasis on improved active transit options supported by a historic citizen-led anti-freeway movement. It has resulted in the construction of several seaways and greenways, such as the Comox-Helmcken Greenway that connects neighborhoods and city amenities through green spaces, blue spaces and bike lanes. Park development has also received a significant portion of the municipal budget (14%), with much attention given to green space and open space protection and the preservation of views to natural landscapes, thus establishing setbacks and sight-lines that encouraged developers to build up and densify the city center while simultaneously financing open space amenities. This densification has been labeled "Vancouverism" (Boddy 2005). The 2010 Winter Olympics further contributed to the spread of Vancouver's green brand and approach, with dozens of new public transit, green infrastructure and new park projects. As a result of land redevelopment, densification and greening, some neighborhoods (as a whole) such as Southeast False Creek have received the LEED platinum designation. Its energy utility, which started operating in 2010, uses captured thermal energy from sewage to heat space and water in the neighborhood buildings. All these projects which make up Vancouver's green brand have been valued at $31 billion (Ryan 2016).

However, Vancouver is consistently ranked as one of the most expensive real estate markets in the world and the most expensive market in Canada (Gaviola 2019). Since the late 1980s, the availability of affordable and social housing in the city has been drastically declining, and the city's homeless population has significantly increased, especially so in the Downtown Eastside. Considerable real estate capital is sourced from foreign owners, particularly from China and Hong Kong, with 19.2% of all condos owned by non-residents of Canada and 6.5% of housing empty or underused (Hager 2017). Furthermore, one in every four homes is valued at over CAD$3 million or more, making it impossible for most middle- and working-class residents to own property or pay increasing property taxes (Gaviola 2019).

Back in 2008, EcoDensity already attempted to respond to Vancouver's affordability crisis by supporting an increased supply of apartment units and single-family homes meant to lower prices through densification. But the program received opposition from community groups who claimed that EcoDensity did little to tackle affordability as non-market housing remains capped at 8.5% (although large projects are required to have 20% affordable housing).

As a means to reduce the housing affordability and scarcity crisis, in 2018 the Province of British Columbia implemented the Additional Property Transfer Tax for Foreign Entities and Taxable Trustees, taxing 20% of the fair market value of the property. As a result, prices in the affluent municipality of West Vancouver have gone down 17% (Pearson 2019). In addition, the province also later implemented a speculation and vacancy tax of 2% of property value for foreign owners. In an effort to offer options to improve housing availability, the province offers an exemption to the foreign ownership vacancy tax by encouraging rental tenancy of the property. With this exemption, many properties have been rented to tenants and the tax mainly affects expensive luxury homes and mega-mansions.

Even with such policy interventions, many Metro Vancouver residents have made calls to pass more stringent anti-speculation, anti-growth housing policies and to ban foreign investment in residential property altogether. Furthermore, the attention to the "foreignness" of these investments has propelled xenophobia and anti-Chinese sentiments throughout the Metro Vancouver region, leaving many Chinese Canadians feeling socially displaced from their greater community.

Conclusion

In May 2020, amid the pandemic, an activist from Via Campesina on the US–Mexico border city of Ciudad Juarez spoke about the impact of COVID-19 on the life, work and health of immigrant farmworkers: "Many of us are not even really 'in the same boat'; we are in the water. As much as we scream for help to those on the boat, they ignore us because they are focused on their own survival". Five years earlier, when Anthropocene-centered narratives and climate change warnings were taking hold, urban political ecologist Erik Swyngedouw wrote: "Many already live *in* the apocalypse, in those places where the intertwining of environmental change and social conditions has already reduced living conditions to 'bare life'" (Swyngedouw 2014). While there is no one "big event" of unsustainability looming over humanity all at once, the activist's metaphor is a strikingly crisp visualization of how urban sustainability unequally plays out in the lives and livelihoods of vulnerable urban residents.

When cities design for sustainability, as we have shown in this book, it is often the most privileged groups that are able to be part of the process and that ultimately reap the benefits. We set out to identify and distill the ten drivers of injustice that maintain and exacerbate this status quo. Inequalities faced by disadvantaged groups (unemployment, education, income, housing security, etc.) are frequently either deemed irrelevant to sustainability or falsely claimed to be resolved by the "trickling down" of sustainability benefits. Just as with COVID-19 and climate change, the wicked and closely related problem of (un)sustainability is at its core a question of justice. In this sense, the question is not simply *how* to sustain, but *what* to sustain. As Miller (Miller 2015, 110) argues, any "innately exploitative system—exploitative of both human beings and natural ecosystems—is sustainable if it can reproduce itself". In defining sustainability, we believe it is essential to first ask: urban sustainability for whom and by whom?

By gathering a broad spectrum of critical literature and our own research, from across the world, including detailed case studies from Europe and

DOI: 10.4324/9781003221425-12

North America and key examples from the Global South, we demonstrate how each driver is a product of historical and ongoing, material, discursive, emergent, and cross-scale conditions and phenomena, that intersect with other injustices. Indeed, it is their interconnectedness and multilayered nature that make sustainability a wicked problem. Our effort to disentangle such patterns relies on linking specific place-based stories to the analysis of global political-economic dynamics, connected environments and climatic changes, to illustrate how drivers of injustice emerge and are in turn challenged and contested.

While the term "driver" may evoke a sense of causality that is mono-directional, the identified drivers operate in cyclical and intersectional ways. In other words, manifestations of injustice are complex phenomena, both the outcomes of drivers and the starting point for new ones. For example, in the case of informal riverfront settlements in climate-sensitive urban regions that are labeled as "at risk", people and whole neighborhoods might be displaced to allow for the implementation of sustainable green/ blue amenities and new real estate. Here, several drivers can be at play as material and livelihood inequalities (Driver 1) meet uneven urban intensification and regeneration (Driver 3), through racialized or ethnically exclusionary processes (Driver 2) and limited citizen participation (Driver 8), resulting in an unequal access to the benefits of urban sustainability (Driver 5). Such processes are often the result of power-knowledge asymmetries (Driver 9) that are reproduced through dominant institutions and their unfit structures and practices (Driver 6), in turn largely driven by the imperative for continuous economic growth and an ideology of neoliberal governance (Driver 10). These intersections are some of many we have drawn through the examples and case studies in this book.

The research presented here makes clear that hastily considering justice as an automatic outcome of sustainability or retrofitting justice according to a vision of sustainability conditioned by the same social hierarchies and inequalities it aims to address risks undermining both justice and sustainability. We call on students, scholars and practitioners of sustainability to move beyond orthodox visions of urban sustainability which are proving "politically unstable, tenuous, and ever blinkering" (Wilson 2015) and to question dominant visions of justice that pursue "shallow" equity through disengaged, top-down and tokenistic participatory schemes or inaccessible redistribution policies.

How, then, can we move forward toward a genuinely sustainable and just urban practice? First, it is essential to expose the contradictions of many green projects and the impacts of profit-driven interests dominated by a white elite. Our research shows that even with safeguards in place, green finance capital is multiplying with no concern for social justice. To truly enact urban justice, urban sustainability must be reparative (Webber et al. 2022; Anguelovski et al. 2020), entailing practices that restore and sustain natural resources while addressing deep-rooted exclusion, discrimination, trauma and broader inequalities, particularly for working-class and racialized residents. Specifically, repairing refers to practices grounded in racialized minorities—especially Black—abolitionist traditions that can restore the sites, relations and institutions that colonization, slavery, capitalism and carceral systems have invisibilized or ruptured (Heynen and Ybarra 2021). Reparations should address harms and traumas produced by unequal urban development, which necessitates new spaces and relations underpinned by care, flourishing, reciprocity and community wealth creation (Ranganathan and Bratman 2021). These principles are aligned with the concept of "reparations ecologies" (Cadieux et al. 2019), which advocates that environmental systems, social and physical infrastructures must be questioned and reassembled along with our societal human relations.

In practice, reparative justice in urban sustainability requires the redistribution of economic and political power through decommodification, whereby neoliberal and growth-driven agendas and the dominance of markets in socioeconomic and ecological relations are dismantled. It requires the crafting of new democratic institutions and the securing of new land and tenure arrangements for historically marginalized groups in cities and beyond. It suggests new organizational and civic arrangements in the form of cooperative enterprises and other member-owned business structures, along with the restriction and limiting of predatory international financial markets, and the progressive taxation of international capital flows. It also underscores the need for more public–non-profit partnerships and the remunicipalization of key resources and infrastructural services, including water, electricity and waste management. These new arrangements will require engagement with the state (to rework bureaucratic infrastructure, question the reliance of public investments on private markets and propose reforms), and beyond the state, to create new spaces of autonomy and self-determination. These arrangements should enable the recognition of a plurality of knowledges around sustainability based on a diversity of experiences and histories (Broto, Westman, and Huang 2021).

These principles are also linked to a deeper consideration of urban abolition ecologies and abolitionist climate and green justice (Heynen 2016; Anguelovski et al. 2021a). Abolitionism—the eradication of systematic and institutionalized oppression and violence that further entrench inequality and exclusion—questions the spatial logics that have shaped urban neighborhoods into sites of environmental toxics, poor access to environmental amenities and enduring ghettoization, discrimination and segregation along lines of race and other axes of social difference, by fighting to abolish such spatial logics and the social relations that create them. As we have discussed throughout the book, processes of exclusion and oppression must be understood as fundamentally intersectional (Cho, Crenshaw, and McCall 2013). In this sense, abolitionist practices must confront the ways in which environmental injustices of toxicity and pollution are compounded by unequal access to housing, increased risk of eviction, healthy food, affordable and networked public transit, safe public and green spaces, and by overall greater exposure to climate risks and impacts and the traumas associated with such inequalities.

Finally, our analysis of ten drivers of urban injustice reveals the need to recenter anti-racism in local and global environmental and environmental justice movements. This means engaging in conversations with radical social movements—from anti-racist, immigrant and indigenous rights groups to feminist and degrowth activists—to share common struggles and generate new spaces of placemaking and activism across all spheres: in the home, workplace, the street, the plaza and the peri-urban. Greater alliances between these agendas would support economic alternatives to resource extraction and depletion, provide social alternatives to enduring colonial and patriarchal patterns of exploitation and discrimination, and prove a more potent force in dismantling the drivers of urban injustice.

References

Abazeri, Mariam. 2022. "Decolonial Feminisms and Degrowth." *Futures* 136: 102902.

Adams, Barbara, and Karen Judd. 2016. "Silos or System? The 2030 Agenda Requires an Integrated Approach to Sustainable Development." *Global Policy Forum Brief* 12: 23.

Adler, David, Pawel Wargan, and Sona Prakash. 2019. "Blueprint for Europe's Just Transition." *The Green New Deal for Europe*. https://report.gndforeurope.com/cms/wp-content/uploads/2020/01/Blueprint-for-Europes-Just-Transition-2nd-Ed.pdf.

Agyeman, Julian, Robert D. Bullard, and Bob Evans. 2002. "Exploring the Nexus: Bringing Together Sustainability, Environmental Justice and Equity." *Space and Polity* 6 (1): 77–90.

Agyeman, Julian, Robert Doyle Bullard, and Bob Evans. 2003. *Just Sustainabilities: Development in an Unequal World*. Cambridge: MIT Press.

Alkon, Alison Hope, and Josh Cadji. 2020. "Sowing Seeds of Displacement: Gentrification and Food Justice in Oakland, CA." *International Journal of Urban and Regional Research* 44 (1): 108–23.

Alkon, Alison Hope, and Julie Guthman. 2017. "The New Food Activism." *Oppisition, Cooperation and Collective Action*. San Francisco: University of California Press Books.

Amorim-Maia, Ana T., Isabelle Anguelovski, Eric Chu, and James Connolly. 2022. "Intersectional Climate Justice: A Conceptual Pathway for Bridging Adaptation Planning, Transformative Action, and Social Equity." *Urban Climate* 41: 101053. https://doi.org/10.1016/j.uclim.2021.101053.

Angel, Shlomo, Jason Parent, Daniel L. Civco, Alexander Blei, and David Potere. 2011. "The Dimensions of Global Urban Expansion: Estimates and Projections for All Countries, 2000–2050." *Progress in Planning* 75 (2): 53–107.

Angelo, Hilary. 2021. *How Green Became Good: Urbanized Nature and the Making of Cities and Citizens*. Chicago: University of Chicago Press.

Anguelovski, Isabelle. 2013. "New Directions in Urban Environmental Justice: Rebuilding Community, Addressing Trauma, and Remaking Place." *Journal of Planning Education and Research* 33 (2): 160–75.

————. 2014. *Neighborhood as Refuge: Community Reconstruction, Place Remaking, and Environmental Justice in the City*. Cambridge: MIT Press.

————. 2016a. "Healthy Food Stores, Greenlining and Food Gentrification: Contesting New Forms of Privilege, Displacement and Locally Unwanted Land Uses in Racially Mixed Neighborhoods." *International Journal of Urban and Regional Research* 39 (6): 1209–30.

————. 2016b. "From Toxic Sites to Parks as (Green) LULUs? New Challenges of Inequity, Privilege, Gentrification, and Exclusion for Urban Environmental Justice." *Journal of Planning Literature* 31 (1): 23–36. https://doi.org/10.1177/0885412215610491.

Anguelovski, Isabelle, Anna Livia Brand, James J. T. Connolly, Esteve Corbera, Panagiota Kotsila, Justin Steil, Melissa Garcia-Lamarca, Margarita Triguero-Mas, Helen Cole, and Francesc Baró. 2020. "Expanding the Boundaries of Justice in Urban Greening Scholarship: Toward an Emancipatory, Antisubordination, Intersectional, and Relational Approach." *Annals of the American Association of Geographers*: 1–27.

Anguelovski, Isabelle, Anna Livia Brand, Malini Ranganathan, and Derek Hyra. 2021a. "Decolonizing the Green City: From Environmental Privilege to Emancipatory Green Justice." *Environmental Justice* 15 (1): 1–11.

Anguelovski, Isabelle, Clara Irazábal-Zurita, and James J. T. Connolly. 2019b. "Grabbed Urban Landscapes: Socio-spatial Tensions in Green Infrastructure Planning in Medellín." *International Journal of Urban and Regional Research* 43 (1): 133–56.

Anguelovski, Isabelle, and James J. T. Connolly. 2021. *The Green City and Social Injustice: 21 Tales from North America and Europe*. Edited by Isabelle Anguelovski and James J. T. Connolly. London: Routledge.

Anguelovski, Isabelle, James J. T. Connolly, Hamil Pearsall, Galia Shokry, Melissa Checker, Juliana Maantay, Kenneth Gould, Tammy Lewis, Andrew Maroko, and J. Timmons Roberts. 2019a. "Opinion: Why Green 'Climate Gentrification' Threatens Poor and Vulnerable Populations." *Proceedings of the National Academy of Sciences* 116 (52): 26139–43.

Anguelovski, Isabelle, James J. T. Connolly, Laia Masip, and Hamil Pearsall. 2018. "Assessing Green Gentrification in Historically Disenfranchised Neighborhoods: A Longitudinal and Spatial Analysis of Barcelona." *Urban Geography* 39 (3): 458–91.

Anguelovski, Isabelle, James J. T. Connolly, Melissa Garcia-Lamarca, Helen Cole, and Hamil Pearsall. 2019c. "New Scholarly Pathways on Green Gentrification: What Does the Urban 'Green Turn' Mean and Where Is It Going?" *Progress in Human Geography* 43 (6): 1064–86.

Anguelovski, Isabelle, and Joan Martínez Alier. 2014. "The 'Environmentalism of the Poor' Revisited: Territory and Place in Disconnected Glocal Struggles." *Ecological Economics* 102: 167–76.

Anguelovski, Isabelle, Linda Shi, Eric Chu, Daniel Gallagher, Kian Goh, Zachary Lamb, Kara Reeve, and Hannah Teicher. 2016. "Equity Impacts of Urban Land Use Planning for Climate Adaptation Critical Perspectives from the Global North and South." *Journal of Planning Education and Research* 36 (3): 333–48.

Anguelovski, Isabelle, Panagiota Kotsila, Dave Moore, and Mick Lennon. 2021b. "Environmental Inequities in Fast-Growing Dublin: Combined Scarcity of Green Space and Affordable Housing for The Liberties." In *The Green City and Social Injustice*, edited by Isabelle Anguelovski and James J. T. Connolly. 200–12. Abingdon, Oxon and New York, NY: Routledge.

Apostolopoulou, Elia, and Panagiota Kotsila. 2021. "Community Gardening in Hellinikon as a Resistance Struggle against Neoliberal Urbanism: Spatial Autogestion and the Right to the City in Post-Crisis Athens, Greece." *Urban Geography* (January): 1–27. https://doi.org/10.1080/02723638.2020.1863621.

Arbaci, Sonia. 2019. *Paradoxes of Segregation: Housing Systems, Welfare Regimes and Ethnic Residential Change in Southern European Cities*. Oxford: Wiley.

Arboleda, Martín. 2016. "Spaces of Extraction, Metropolitan Explosions: Planetary Urbanization and the Commodity Boom in Latin America." *International Journal of Urban and Regional Research* 40 (1): 96–112.

Argüelles, Lucía. 2021a. "Enacting a Rail-to-Park Project in Valencia Parc Central or the Actual Construction of Green Gentrification." *The Green City and Social Injustice* 61–72.

———. 2021b. "Growing Farming Heroes? Politics of Imaginaries within Farmer Training Programs in California." *Annals of the American Association of Geographers* 111 (5): 1385–402.

———. 2021c. "Privileged Socionatures and Naturalization of Privilege: Untangling Environmental Privilege Dimensions." *The Professional Geographer* 73 (4): 650–61. https://doi.org/10.1080/00330124.2021.1924804.

Argüelles, Lucía, Isabelle Anguelovski, and Elizabeth Dinnie. 2017. "Power and Privilege in Alternative Civic Practices: Examining Imaginaries of Change and Embedded Rationalities in Community Economies." *Geoforum* 86: 30–41.

Argüelles, Lucía, Isabelle Anguelovski, and Filka Sekulova. 2018. "How to Survive: Artificial Quality Food Schemes and New Forms of Rule for Farmers in Direct Marketing Strategies." *Journal of Rural Studies* 62: 10–20. https://doi.org/10.1016/j.jrurstud.2018.06.005.

Armiero, Marco, Thanos Andritsos, Stefania Barca, Rita Brás, Sergio Ruiz Cauyela, Çağdaş Dedeoğlu, Marica Di Pierri, Lúcia de Oliveira Fernandes, Filippo Gravagno, and Laura Greco. 2019. "Toxic Bios: Toxic Autobiographies—A Public Environmental Humanities Project." *Environmental Justice* 12 (1): 7–11.

Armiero, Marco, and Giacomo D'Alisa. 2012. "Rights of Resistance: The Garbage Struggles for Environmental Justice in Campania, Italy." *Capitalism Nature Socialism* 23 (4): 52–68.

Arnstein, Sherry R. 1969. "A Ladder of Citizen Participation." *Journal of the American Institute of Planners* 35 (4): 216–24. https://doi.org/10.1080/01944366908977225.

Asante-Muhammad, Dedrick, Chuck Collins, Josh Hoxie, and Emanuel Nieves. 2017. "The Road to Zero Wealth: How the Racial Wealth Divide Is Hollowing out America's Middle Class." *Prosperity Now*, September.

Atkinson, Rowland. 2018. "London's Extraordinary Surplus of Empty Apartments Revealed." *The Conversation*, October 28. https://theconversation.com/londons-extraordinary-surplus-of-empty-luxury-apartments-revealed-97947.

Bailey, Nick, Wouter P. C. van Gent, and Sako Musterd. 2017. "Remaking Urban Segregation: Processes of Income Sorting and Neighbourhood Change." *Population, Space and Place* 23 (3): e2013.

Bailey, Zinzi D., Nancy Krieger, Madina Agénor, Jasmine Graves, Natalia Linos, and Mary T. Bassett. 2017. "Structural Racism and Health Inequities in the USA: Evidence and Interventions." *The Lancet* 389 (10077): 1453–63. https://doi.org/10.1016/S0140-6736(17)30569-X.

Barcegol, Remi de, and Shankare Gowda. 2020. "Waste in the Urban Margins. The Example of Dehli's Waste Pickers." In *Living in the Margins in Mainland China, Hong Kong and India*, edited by Wing Chung Ho and Florence Padovani, 1st ed., 23. Routledge. https://doi.org/https://doi.org/10.4324/9781003037873.

Barcelona City Council. 2013. "Barcelona Green Infrastructure and Biodiversity Plan 2020." Accessed March 17, 2022. https://ajuntament.barcelona.cat/ecologiaurbana/sites/default/files/Barcelona green infrastructure and biodiversity plan 2020.pdf.

Barcelona City Council. 2018. "Climate Plan 2018–2030." Accessed March 17, 2022. www.barcelona.cat/barcelona-pel-clima/sites/default/files/documents/plan_clima_juny_ok.pdf.

Baró, F., and I. Anguelovski. 2021. "Will 'Extraordinary Gardens' and Social Housing Ensure Nantes is Green and Affordable for All?" In *The Green City and Social Injustice: 21 Tales from North America and Europe*, edited by Isabelle Anguelovski and James J. T. Connolly. London: Routledge.

Baró, F., Lydia Chaparro, Erik Gómez-Baggethun, Johannes Langemeyer, David J. Nowak, and Jaume Terradas. 2014. "Contribution of Ecosystem Services to Air Quality and Climate Change Mitigation Policies: The Case of Urban Forests in Barcelona, Spain." *Ambio* 43 (4): 466–79.

Barry, Janice, and Julian Agyeman. 2020. "On Belonging and Becoming in the Settler-Colonial City: Co-Produced Futurities, Placemaking, and Urban Planning in the United States." *Journal of Race, Ethnicity and the City* 1 (1–2): 22–41. https://doi.org/10.1080/26884674.2020.1793703.

BBAR (Building Bridges Across the River). 2018. *11th Street Bridge Park's Equitable Development Plan*. Washington, DC: BBAR.

BCNUEJ. 2021. *Urban Green Justice Policy and Planning Toolkit. Barcelona Lab for Urban Environmental Justice and Sustainability*. Edited by E. Oscilowicz, I. Anguelovski, and H. Cole. www.bcnuej.org/wp-content/uploads/2021/04/Toolkit-Urban-Green-Justice.pdf.

BCNUEJ. 2022. "The Green Divide, Poblenou Neighborhood. Interactive Web documentary. Barcelona Lab for Urban Environmental Justice and Sustainability." www.bcnuej.org/greendivide/#Poblenou_-_Barcelona.

Beall, Jo, and Sean Fox. 2009. *Cities and Development*. London: Routledge.

Bigger, Patrick, and Nate Millington. 2020. "Getting Soaked? Climate Crisis, Adaptation Finance, and Racialized Austerity." *Environment and Planning E: Nature and Space* 3 (3): 601–23.

Blok, Anders. 2020. "Urban Green Gentrification in an Unequal World of Climate Change." *Urban Studies* 57 (14): 2803–16.

Boddy, Trevor. 2005. "INSIGHT: Vancouverism vs. Lower Manhattanism: Shaping the High Density City." *ArchNewsNOW.com*, September 20. www.archnewsnow.com/features/Feature177.htm.

Bonnedahl, Karl Johan, Pasi Heikkurinen, and Jouni Paavola. 2022. "Strongly Sustainable Development Goals: Overcoming Distances Constraining Responsible Action." *Environmental Science & Policy* 129: 150–58.

Boone, Christopher G., Geoffrey L. Buckley, J. Morgan Grove, and Chona Sister. 2009. "Parks and People: An Environmental Justice Inquiry in Baltimore, Maryland." *Annals of the Association of American Geographers* 99 (4): 767–87. https://doi.org/10.1080/00045600903102949.

Boone, Christopher G., Mary L. Cadenasso, J. Morgan Grove, Kirsten Schwarz, and Geoffrey L. Buckley. 2010. "Landscape, Vegetation Characteristics, and Group Identity in an Urban and Suburban Watershed: Why the 60s Matter." *Urban Ecosystems* 13 (3): 255–71.

Borowy, Iris. 2019. "Sustainability and Redistribution." In *What Next for Sustainable Development?*, edited by Meadowcroft, James, David Banister, Erling Holden, Oluf Langhelle, Kristin Linnerud, and Geoffrey Gilpin. Cheltenham and Masachussets: Edward Elgar Publishing.

Bouzarovski, Stefan, Jan Frankowski, and Sergio Tirado Herrero. 2018. "Lowcarbon Gentrification: When Climate Change Encounters Residential Displacement." *International Journal of Urban and Regional Research* 42 (5): 845–63.

Brand, Ulrich, and Markus Wissen. 2021. *The Imperial Mode of Living: Everyday Life and the Ecological Crisis of Capitalism*. London and New York: Verso Books.

Brenner, Neil. 2018. "Debating Planetary Urbanization: For an Engaged Pluralism." *Environment and Planning D: Society and Space* 36 (3): 570–90.

Bridge, Gary, Tim Butler, and Loretta Lees. 2011. *Mixed Communities: Gentrification By Stealth?* Bristol: Policy Press. https://doi.org/10.1332/policypress/9781847424938.001.0001.

Broto, Vanesa Castán, Linda Westman, and Ping Huang. 2021. "Reparative Innovation for Urban Climate Adaptation." *Journal of the British Academy* 9 (Supplement 9): 205–18.

Bryant, Bunyan, and Paul Mohai. 2019. *Race and the Incidence of Environmental Hazards: A Time for Discourse*. 2nd ed. New York: Routledge.

Bui, Lily. 2018. "Rewiring Puerto Rico: Power and Empowerment after Hurricane Maria." *Alternautas* 5 (2). www.alternautas.net/blog/2018/10/29/rewiring-puerto-rico-power-and-empowerment-after-hurricane-maria.

Bulkeley, Harriet A., Vanesa Castán Broto, and Gareth A. S. Edwards. 2015. *An Urban Politics of Climate Change: Experimentation and the Governing of Socio-Technical Transitions*. London: Routledge.

Bulkeley, Harriet A., and Peter Newell. 2015. *Governing Climate Change*. London: Routledge.

Bunce, Susannah. 2017. *Sustainability Policy, Planning and Gentrification in Cities*. London: Routledge.

Busch, Andrew M. 2017. *City in a Garden: Environmental Transformations and Racial Justice in Twentieth-Century*. Austin, TX: UNC Press Books.

Byrne, Jason. 2012. "When Green Is White: The Cultural Politics of Race, Nature and Social Exclusion in a Los Angeles Urban National Park." *Geoforum* 43 (3): 595–611.

Cadieux, Kirsten Valentine, Stephen Carpenter, Alex Liebman, Renata Blumberg, and Bhaskar Upadhyay. 2019. "Reparation Ecologies: Regimes of Repair in Populist Agroecology." *Annals of the American Association of Geographers* 109 (2): 644–60.

Calavita, Nico, and Amador Ferrer. 2004. "Behind Barcelona's Success Story—Citizen Movements and Planners' Power." In *Transforming Barcelona: The Renewal of a European Metropolis*, edited by Tim Marshall, 48–66. London: Routledge.

Calderón-Argelich, Amalia, Stefania Benetti, Isabelle Anguelovski, James J. T. Connolly, Johannes Langemeyer, and Francesc Baró. 2021. "Tracing and Building Up Environmental Justice Considerations in the Urban Ecosystem Service Literature: A Systematic Review." *Landscape and Urban Planning* 214: 104130.

Camprubí, Lluís, Davide Malmusi, Roshanak Mehdipanah, Laia Palència, Agnes Molnar, Carles Muntaner, and Carme Borrell. 2016. "Façade Insulation Retrofitting Policy Implementation Process and Its Effects on Health Equity Determinants: A Realist Review." *Energy Policy* 91: 304–14. https://doi.org/10.1016/j.enpol.2016.01.016.

Caniglia, Beth Schaefer, Manuel Vallée, and Beatrice Frank. 2016. *Resilience, Environmental Justice and the City*. London: Routledge.

Caprotti, Federico, Cecilia Springer, and Nichola Harmer. 2015. " 'Eco' For Whom? Envisioning Eco-urbanism in the Sino-Singapore Tianjin Eco-city, China." *International Journal of Urban and Regional Research* 39 (3): 495–517.

Castán Broto, Vanesa, and Linda Westman. 2019. *Urban Sustainability and Justice: Just Sustainabilities and Environmental Planning*. London: Bloomsbury Publishing.

Cho, Sumi, Kimberlé Williams Crenshaw, and Leslie McCall. 2013. "Toward a Field of Intersectionality Studies: Theory, Applications, and Praxis." *Signs: Journal of Women in Culture and Society* 38 (4): 785–810.

Chu, Eric. 2016. "The Political Economy of Urban Climate Adaptation and Development Planning in Surat, India." *Environment and Planning C: Government and Policy* 34 (2): 281–98.

Chu, Eric, Isabelle Anguelovski, and JoAnn Carmin. 2015. "Inclusive Approaches to Urban Climate Adaptation Planning and Implementation in the Global South." *Climate Policy*, no. ahead-of-print: 1–21.

———. 2016. "Inclusive Approaches to Urban Climate Adaptation Planning and Implementation in the Global South." *Climate Policy* 16 (3): 372–92.

City of Boston. n.d. "Climate Ready East Boston." Accessed February 03, 2022. https://www.boston.gov/departments/environment/climate-ready-east-boston

City of Portland. n.d. "Displacement in North and Northeast Portland: An Historical Overview." Accessed March 16, 2022. www.portlandoregon.gov/phb/article/655460.

Cocola-Gant, Agustin, and Antonio Lopez-Gay. 2020. "Transnational Gentrification, Tourism and the Formation of 'Foreign Only' Enclaves in Barcelona." *Urban Studies* 57 (15): 3025–43.

Cole, Helen. 2021. "West Dallas: The 'Nowhere' That Became 'Somewhere'." In *The Green City and Social Injustice: 21 Tales From North America and Europe*, edited by Isabelle Anguelovski and James J. T. Connolly, 88–99. London: Routledge.

Cole, Helen, Raul Reyes Jr., and Kathryn Bazan. 2021. *Communities of Color Are Leading the Fight for a Cleaner West Dallas*. Green Inequalities. www.bcnuej.org/2021/09/13/communities-of-color-are-leading-the-fight-for-a-cleaner-west-.

Cole, Helen V. S., Isabelle Anguelovski, Francesc Baró, Melissa García-Lamarca, Panagiota Kotsila, Carmen Pérez del Pulgar, Galia Shokry, and Margarita Triguero-Mas. 2020. "The COVID-19 Pandemic: Power and Privilege, Gentrification, and Urban Environmental Justice in the Global North." *Cities & Health* (July): 1–5. https://doi.org/10.1080/23748834.2020.1785176.

Cole, Helen V. S., Isabelle Anguelovski, James J. T Connolly, Melissa García-Lamarca, Carmen Perez-del-Pulgar, Galia Shokry, and Margarita Triguero-Mas. 2021. "Adapting the Environmental Risk Transition Theory for Urban Health Inequities: An Observational Study Examining Complex Environmental Riskscapes in Seven Neighborhoods in Global North Cities." *Social Science & Medicine* 277: 113907. https://doi.org/10.1016/j.socscimed.2021.113907.

Cole, Helen V. S., Melisa Garcia Lamarca, James J. T. Connolly, and Isabelle Anguelovski. 2017. "Are Green Cities Healthy and Equitable? Unpacking the Relationship Between Health, Green Space and Gentrification." *Journal of Epidemiol Community Health* 71 (11): 1118–21.

Collins, Cory. 2018. "What Is White Privilege, Really?" *Learning for Justice, Issue* 60 (Fall). www.learningforjustice.org/magazine/fall-2018/what-is-white-privilege-really.

Collins, Timothy W. 2010. "Marginalization, Facilitation, and the Production of Unequal Risk: The 2006 Paso Del Norte Floods." *Antipode* 42 (2): 258–88.

Comelli, Thaisa, Isabelle Anguelovski, and Eric Chu. 2018. "Socio-Spatial Legibility, Discipline, and Gentrification Through Favela Upgrading in Rio de Janeiro." *City* 22 (5–6): 633–56. https://doi.org/10.1080/13604813.2018.1549205.

Conde, Marta, Giacomo D'Alisa, and Filka Sekulova. 2022. "When Greening Is Not Degrowth: Cost-Shifting Insights." In *Post-Growth Planning*, edited by Federico Savini, António Ferreira, Kim von Schönfeld, 19–31. New York: Routledge.

Connolly, James J. T. 2018. *From Systems Thinking to Systemic Action: Social Vulnerability and the Institutional Challenge of Urban Resilience*. Los Angeles, CA: SAGE Publications Sage.

———. 2019. "From Jacobs to the Just City: A Foundation for Challenging Green Planning Orthodoxy." *Cities* 91: 64–70.

Connolly, James J. T., and Isabelle Anguelovski. 2021. "Three Histories of Greening and Whiteness in American Cities." *Frontiers in Ecology and Evolution*. www.frontiersin.org/article/10.3389/fevo.2021.621783.

Connolly, James J. T., and Mateus Lira. 2021. "A New Shade of Green: From Historic Environmental Inequalities Over Green Amenities to Exclusive Green Growth in Austin." In *The Green City and Social Injustice: 21 Tales from North America and Europe*, edited by Isabelle Anguelovski and James J. T. Connolly. London: Routledge.

Cook, Ian R., and Erik Swyngedouw. 2012. "Cities, Social Cohesion and the Environment: Towards a Future Research Agenda." *Urban Studies* 49 (9): 1959–79.

Cook, Mitchell J., and Eric K. Chu. 2018. "Between Policies, Programs, and Projects: How Local Actors Steer Domestic Urban Climate Adaptation Finance in India." In *Climate Change in Cities*, edited by Sara Hughes, Eric K. Chu, Susan G. Mason, 255–77. Cham: Springer.

Corburn, Jason. 2005. *Street Science. Community Knowledge and Environmental Health Justice*. Cambridge: MIT Press.

Cornwall, Andrea. 2008. "Unpacking 'Participation': Models, Meanings and Practices." *Community Development Journal* 43 (3): 269–83. https://doi.org/10.1093/cdj/bsn010.

Couch, Chris, and Charles Fraser. 2003. "Introduction: The European Context and Theoretical Framework." In *Urban Regeneration in Europe*, edited by Chris Couch, Charles Fraser, and Susan Percy, 1–16. Oxford: Blackwell.

Couch, Chris, Charles Fraser, and Susan Percy. 2003. *Urban Regeneration in Europe*. Oxford: Blackwell.

Couch, Chris, Olivier Sykes, and Wolfgang Börstinghaus. 2011. "Thirty Years of Urban Regeneration in Britain, Germany and France: The Importance of Context and Path Dependency." *Progress in Planning* 75 (1): 1–52.

Cowley, Joe, John Kiely, and Dave Collins. 2016. "Unravelling the Glasgow Effect: The Relationship between Accumulative Bio-Psychosocial Stress, Stress Reactivity and Scotland's Health Problems." *Preventive Medicine Reports* 4: 370–75.

Cruz-Martínez, Gibrán, Melissa Fernández Arrigoitia, Janialy Ortiz Camacho, and Patria Roman-Velazquez. 2018. "Introduction to the Special Issue: 'The Making of Caribbean Not-so-Natural Disasters.'" *Alternautas* 5 (2). www.alternautas.net/blog/2018/9/7/introduction-to-the-special-issue-the-making-of-caribbean-not-so-natural-disasters.

Curran, Winifred, and Trina Hamilton. 2017. *Just Green Enough: Urban Development and Environmental Gentrification*. New York: Routledge.

D'alisa, Giacomo, Federico Demaria, and Giorgos Kallis. 2014. *Degrowth: A Vocabulary for a New Era*. London: Routledge.

Daly, Herman E. 1996. *Beyond Growth: The Economics of Sustainable Development*. Boston: Beacon Press.

Daly, Jonathan. 2020. "Superkilen: Exploring the Human—Nonhuman Relations of Intercultural Encounter." *Journal of Urban Design* 25 (1): 65–85. https://doi.org/10.1080/13574809.2019.1622409.

Demaria, Federico, Francois Schneider, Filka Sekulova, and Joan Martinez-Alier. 2013. "What Is Degrowth? From an Activist Slogan to a Social Movement." *Environmental Values* 22 (2): 191–215.

Di Paola, Lucia. 2021. "Milan's Private Vertical Forests vs. Horizontal Urban Greening." In *The Green City and Social Injustice: 21 Tales from North America and Europe*, edited by Isabelle Anguelovski and James J. T. Connolly, 88–99. London: Routledge.

Dodman, D., B. Hayward, M. Pelling, V. Castan Broto, W. Chow, E. Chu, R. Dawson, et al. 2022. "Cities, Settlements and Key Infrastructure." In *Climate Change 2022: Impacts, Adaptation, and Vulnerability. Contribution of Working Group II to the Sixth Assessment Report of the Intergovernmental Panel on Climate*

Change, edited by H.-O. Pörtner, D. C. Roberts, M. Tignor, E. S. Poloczanska, K. Mintenbeck, and A. Aleg. Cambridge University Press.

Doshi, Sapana. 2017. "Embodied Urban Political Ecology: Five Propositions." *Area* 49 (1): 125–28.

Dublin City Council. 2015. "The Liberties Greening Strategy." *Dublin City Council.* Accessed May 05 2019. https://www.dublincity.ie/sites/default/files/2021-02/liberties-greening-strategy_0.pdf

Duncan, Dustin T., and Ichiro Kawachi. 2018. "Neighborhoods and Health: A Progress Report", edited by Dustin T. Duncan and Ichiro Kawachi. 2nd ed. Oxford University Press. https://doi.org/10.1093/oso/9780190843496.001.0001.

Ecolise. 2021. "ECOLISE Council Issues Statement Regarding the Appeals Board Review of the 'Report on Allegations of Gross Misconduct'." Accessed November 24, 2021. www.ecolise.eu/ecolise-council-issues-statement-regarding-the-appeals-board-review-of-the-report-on-allegations-of-gross-misconduct/.

Eisenhauer, David C. 2021. "The Battle for the Boardwalk: Racial Formations in a Segregated Coastal Resort." *Geoforum* 126: 403–11.

Ellis, Rowan. 2011. "Who's Participation? Who's Sustainability? A Critical Analysis of Initiatives for Urban Sustainability in India." *Scottish Geographical Journal* 127 (3): 193–208.

Escobar, Arturo. 1995. "Encountering Development: The Making and Unmaking of the Third World." *Princeton Studies in Culture/Power/History*. Princeton University Press. Princeton. New Jersey.

EUROSTAT. 2021. *Housing in Europe. 2021 Interactive Edition.* EUROSTAT. https://ec.europa.eu/eurostat/cache/digpub/housing/index.html?lang=en.

Ewing, Reid. 1997. "Is Los Angeles-Style Sprawl Desirable?" *Journal of the American Planning Association* 63 (1): 107–26.

Ewing, Reid, Tom Schmid, Richard Killingsworth, Amy Zlot, and Stephen Raudenbush. 2003. "Relationship between Urban Sprawl and Physical Activity, Obesity, and Morbidity." *American Journal of Health Promotion* 18 (1): 47–57.

Fainstein, Susan S. 2014. "The Just City." *International Journal of Urban Sciences* 18 (1): 1–18.

Finney, Carolyn. 2014. *Black Faces, White Spaces: Reimagining the Relationship of African Americans to the Great Outdoors*. Chapel Hill: UNC Press Books.

Florida, Richard. 2002. *The Rise of the Creative Class: And How It's Transforming Work, Leisure, Community and Everyday Life.* New York: Basic Books.

Foster, Sheila. 1998. "Justice From the Ground up: Distributive Inequities, Grassroots Resistance, and the Transformative Politics of the Environmental Justice Movement." *California Law Review* 86 (4): 775. https://doi.org/10.2307/3481140.

Foucault, Michel. 1980. "Two Lectures." In *Power/Knowledge: Selected Interviews and Other Writings, 1972–1977*, edited by Colin Gordon. New York: Pantheon.

Frantzeskaki, Niki, Adina Dumitru, Isabelle Anguelovski, Flor Avelino, Matthew Bach, Benjamin Best, Constanze Binder, Jake Barnes, Giuseppe Carrus, and Markus Egermann. 2016. "Elucidating the Changing Roles of Civil Society in Urban Sustainability Transitions." *Current Opinion in Environmental Sustainability* 22: 41–50.

Fraser, Nancy. 2005. *Reframing Justice*. Drenthe: Uitgeverij Van Gorcum.

Fricker, Miranda. 2007. *Epistemic Injustice: Power and the Ethics of Knowing*. Oxford: Oxford University Press.

Fronteira, Inês, Mohsin Sidat, João Paulo Magalhães, Fernando Passos Cupertino de Barros, António Pedro Delgado, Tiago Correia, Cláudio Tadeu Daniel-Ribeiro, and Paulo Ferrinho. 2021. "The SARS-CoV-2 Pandemic: A Syndemic Perspective." *One Health* 12: 100228. https://doi.org/10.1016/j.onehlt.2021. 100228.

Funtowicz, Silvio O., and Jerome R. Ravetz. 1993. "The Emergence of Post-Normal Science." In *Science, Politics and Morality*, edited by René Schomberg, 85–123. Dordrecht: Springer.

Future Climate Info. n.d. "The Toxic Burn." https://futureclimateinfo.com/the-toxic-burn/.

Gabriel, Nathaniel. 2016. " 'No Place for Wilderness': Urban Parks and the Assembling of Neoliberal Urban Environmental Governance." *Urban Forestry & Urban Greening* 19: 278–84.

Garcia-Lamarca, Melissa, Isabelle Anguelovski, Helen V. S. Cole, James J. T. Connolly, Lucía Argüelles, Francesc Baró, Stephanie Loveless, Carmen Perez del Pulgar Frowein, and Galia Shokry. 2021. "Urban Green Boosterism and City Affordability: For Whom Is the 'Branded' Green City?" *Urban Studies* 58 (1): 90–112.

García-Lamarca, Melissa, Isabelle Anguelovski, Helen V. S. Cole, James J. T. Connolly, Carmen Pérez-del-Pulgar, Galia Shokry, and Margarita Triguero-Mas. 2022. "Urban Green Grabbing: Residential Real Estate Developers Discourse and Practice in Gentrifying Global North Neighborhoods." *Geoforum* 128: 1–10.

Garcia-Lamarca, Melissa, and Neil Gray. 2020. "What Will Glasgow's Smart Canal Mean for Its Historically Deprived Communities?" *BCNUEJ, Green Inequalities*, December 2020. www.bcnuej.org/2020/12/02/what-will-glasgows-smart-canal-mean-for-its-historically-deprived-communities/.

———. 2022. "Land Remediation in Glasgow's East End. A 'Sustainability Fix' for Whose Benefit?" In *The Green City and Social Injustice. 21 Tales from North America and Europe*, edited by Isabelle Anguelovski and James J. T. Connolly. Routledge. https://doi.org/10.4324/9781003183273.

García-Lamarca, Melissa, and Sara Ullström. 2022. " 'Everyone Wants This Market to Grow': The Affective Post-Politics of Municipal Green Bonds." *Environment and Planning E: Nature and Space* 5 (1): 207–24.

Garrard, Jan, Susan Handy, and Jennifer Dill. 2012. "Women and Cycling." *City Cycling* 2012: 211–34.

Gaviola, Anne. 2019. "Canada's Out-Of-Control Rental Market Is Getting Worse in 2019." *Vice*, January 3. www.vice.com/en/article/j5zzxx/canadas-out-of-control-rental-market-is-getting-worse-in-2019.

Ghertner, Delhi D. Asher. 2010. "Green Evictions: Environmental Discourses of a 'Slum-Free' Delhi." In *Global Political Ecology*, edited by Richard Peet, Paul Robbins, Michael Watts, 159–80. London: Routledge.

Glasgow City Council. 2020. *Funding of Programme to Reduce Vacant and Derelict Land in Glasgow Approved*. Glasgow: Glasgow City Council.

Gould, K. A., and T. L. Lewis. 2016. *Green Gentrification: Urban Sustainability and the Struggle for Environmental Justice.* London: Routledge.

Gradozashtnyi Petersburg. "Митинг Зеленой коалиции: борьба за зеленое пространство и свободу." Accessed November 19, 2021. https://protect812.com/ 2019/03/18/miting-zelenoy-koalizii-2019/.

Grandinetti, T. 2019. "Urban Aloha 'aina: Kaka 'ako and a Decolonized Right to the City. Settler Colon." *Stud* 9 (2).

Gray, Neil, and Gerry Mooney. 2011. "Glasgow's New Urban Frontier: 'Civilising' the Population of 'Glasgow East.'" *City* 15 (1): 4–24.

Graziani, Terra, Joel Montano, Ananya Roy, and Pamela Stephens. 2022. "Property, Personhood, and Police: The Making of Race and Space through Nuisance Law." *Antipode* 54 (2): 439–61.

Grossmann, Katrin, James J. T. Connolly, Małgorzata Dereniowska, Giulio Mattioli, Luca Nitschke, Nicola Thomas, and Anaïs Varo. 2021. "From Sustainable Development to Social-Ecological Justice: Addressing Taboos and Naturalizations in Order to Shift Perspective." *Environment and Planning E: Nature and Space* 25148486211029428.

Grove, Morgan, Laura Ogden, Steward Pickett, Chris Boone, Geoff Buckley, Dexter H. Locke, Charlie Lord, and Billy Hall. 2018. "The Legacy Effect: Understanding How Segregation and Environmental Injustice Unfold over Time in Baltimore." *Annals of the American Association of Geographers* 108 (2): 524–37.

Haberl, Helmut, Dominik Wiedenhofer, Doris Virág, Gerald Kalt, Barbara Plank, Paul Brockway, Tomer Fishman, Daniel Hausknost, Fridolin Krausmann, and Bartholomäus Leon-Gruchalski. 2020. "A Systematic Review of the Evidence on Decoupling of GDP, Resource Use and GHG Emissions, Part II: Synthesizing the Insights." *Environmental Research Letters* 15 (6): 65003.

Hager, Mike. 2017. "Vancouver Has the Highest Proportion of Empty, Underused Homes in 35 Years." *The Globe and Mail*, February 8. www.theglobeandmail. com/news/british-columbia/vancouver-has-the-highest-ratio-of-empty-under used-homes-in-35-years/article33961876/.

van Ham, Maarten, Tiit Tammaru, Rūta Ubarevičienė, and Heleen Janssen. 2021. "Rising Inequalities and a Changing Social Geography of Cities. An Introduction to the Global Segregation Book." In *Urban Socio-Economic Segregation and Income Inequality : A Global Perspective*, edited by Maarten van Ham, Tiit Tammaru, Rūta Ubarevičienė, and Heleen Janssen. Springer Nature. https://doi. org/10.1007/978-3-030-64569-4.

Hanaček, Ksenija, Brototi Roy, Sofia Avila, and Giorgos Kallis. 2020. "Ecological Economics and Degrowth: Proposing a Future Research Agenda from the Margins." *Ecological Economics* 169: 106495. https://doi.org/https://doi.org/10.1016/ j.ecolecon.2019.106495.

Haraway, Donna. 1988. "Situated Knowledges: The Science Question in Feminism and the Privilege of Partial Perspective." *Feminist Studies* 14 (3): 575–99.

Harvey, David. 2007. *A Brief History of Neoliberalism.* Oxford: Oxford University Press.

———. 2014. *Seventeen Contradictions and the End of Capitalism.* Oxford: Oxford University Press.

Heerden, Adam David van. 2015. *Valuing Waste and Wasting Value: Rethinking Planning with Informality by Learning from Skarrelers in Cape Town's Southern Suburbs.* University of Cape Town. http://hdl.handle.net/11427/18201.

Hegde, Samarth. 2020. "Does Asthma Make COVID-19 Worse?" *Nature Reviews Immunology* 20 (6): 352. https://doi.org/10.1038/s41577-020-0324-3.

Herz, Marcus. 2016. " 'Then We Offer Them a New Project'—the Production of Projects in Social Work Conducted by Civil Society in Sweden." *Journal of Civil Society* 12 (4): 365–79. https://doi.org/10.1080/17448689.2016.1232782.

Hesse, Barnor. 2007. "Racialized Modernity: An Analytics of White Mythologies." *Ethnic and Racial Studies* 30 (4): 643–63. https://doi.org/10.1080/014 19870701356064.

Heynen, Nik. 2016. "Urban Political Ecology II: The Abolitionist Century." *Progress in Human Geography* 40 (6): 839–45.

Heynen, Nik, and Megan Ybarra. 2021. "On Abolition Ecologies and Making 'Freedom as a Place.'" *Antipode* 53 (1): 21–35. https://doi.org/https://doi.org/10.1111/anti.12666.

Hickel, Jason. 2017. *The Divide: A Brief Guide to Global Inequality and Its Solutions.* London: Penguin Random House.

Hickel, Jason, and Giorgos Kallis. 2020. "Is Green Growth Possible?" *New Political Economy* 25 (4): 469–86.

Hodkinson, Stuart. 2012. "The New Urban Enclosures." *City* 16 (5): 500–18.

Holm, Eric Joseph van. 2019. "Unequal Cities, Unequal Participation: The Effect of Income Inequality on Civic Engagement." *The American Review of Public Administration* 49 (2): 135–44.

Hörschelmann, K., A. Werner, S. Hildebrandt, and Y. Lazova. 2017. "Naturvation Project—Case Study Report." Leipzig.

Hoyt, Lorlene. 2006. "Importing Ideas: The Transnational Transfer of Urban Revitalization Policy." *International Journal of Public Administration* 29 (1–3): 221–43.

Iacovino, Zoe, Whytne Stevens, and Lily Song. 2021. "Black Belt: A Data Narrative For Co-Design Field Lab: Black Belt Study for the Green New Deal." *StoryMaps Online.* Accessed May 13 2020. https://storymaps.arcgis.com/stories/ffc8388080b944c3ba1bb65c8ee4bffe.

Integrated Development Plan (IDP) for the Hellenikon. 2017. Lamda Development for Hellenikon SA (printed version).

Immergluck, Dan. 2009. "Large Redevelopment Initiatives, Housing Values and Gentrification: The Case of the Atlanta Beltline." *Urban Studies* 46 (8): 1723–45.

Immergluck, Dan, and Tharunya Balan. 2018. "Sustainable for Whom? Green Urban Development, Environmental Gentrification, and the Atlanta Beltline." *Urban Geography* 39 (4): 546–62.

IPCC. 2022. "Climate Change 2022: Impacts, Adaptation and Vulnerability. Contribution of Working Group II to the Sixth Assessment Report of the Intergovernmental Panel on Climate Change." www.ipcc.ch/report/ar6/wg2/.

Isin, E. F. 2000. "Introduction: Democracy, Citizenship and the City." In *Democracy, Citizenship and the Global City,* edited by E. F. Isin, 1–21. London: Routledge.

ISSC/UNESCO. 2013. *World Social Science Report 2013: Changing Global Environments*. Paris: UNESCO & Organisation for Economic Co-operation and Development.

Jacob, Klaus, Anna-Lena Guske, Irene Antoni-Komar, Simon Funcke, Tim Gruchmann, Josefa Kny, Elias Naber, Chantal Ruppert-Winkel, Philipp Christopher Sauer, and Klara Helene Stumpf. 2019. "Governance for the Sustainable Economy: Institutional Innovation from the Bottom Up?" *GAIA-Ecological Perspectives for Science and Society* 28 (1): 204–9.

Jaeger, Joel, Tom Cyrs, and Kevin Kennedy. 2019. "As Trump Steps Away from Paris Climate Agreement, U.S. States, Cities and Businesses Step Up." *World Resources Institute*, October 23. www.wri.org/insights/trump-steps-away-paris-climate-agreement-us-states-cities-and-businesses-step.

Janoušková, Svatava. 2013. "Implementation of an Evaluation System—an Indicator Set—in the Healthy City of Chrudim, Czech Republic. September, Charles University." Accessed March 17, 2022. https://neweconomics.org/uploads/images/2018/01/WP3-case-study-Chrudim.pdf.

Jargowsky, Paul A. 2002. "Sprawl, Concentration of Poverty, and Urban Inequality." *Urban Sprawl: Causes, Consequences, and Policy Responses*: 39–72.

Jeffrey, Alex, Lynn Staeheli, and David J Marshall. 2018. "Rethinking the Spaces of Civil Society." In *Political Geography*. 67: 111–14.

Jessop, Bob. 2002. "Liberalism, Neoliberalism, and Urban Governance: A State—Theoretical Perspective." *Antipode* 34 (3): 452–72.

Johnson, Janet Elise, and Aino Saarinen. 2011. "Assessing Civil Society in Putin's Russia: The Plight of Women's Crisis Centers." *Communist and Post-Communist Studies* 44 (1): 41–52. https://doi.org/10.1016/j.postcomstud.2011.01.002.

Kaika, Maria. 2017. "'Don't Call Me Resilient Again!' The New Urban Agenda as Immunology . . . Or . . . What Happens When Communities Refuse to Be Vaccinated with 'Smart Cities' and Indicators." *Environment and Urbanization* 29 (1): 89–102.

Kallis, Giorgos, Michael Kalush, Hugh O'Flynn, Jack Rossiter, and Nicholas Ashford. 2013. "'Friday off': Reducing Working Hours in Europe." *Sustainability* 5 (4): 1545–67.

Katona, A. 2018. "Winnipeg." Naturvation Case Stury Working Paper.

Keating, Cecilia. 2019. "Did a Green Development Project Drive Up the Rent in a Montreal Neighbourhood?" *Canada's National Observer*, January 23, 2019. www.nationalobserver.com/2019/01/23/news/did-green-development-project-drive-rent-montreal-neighbourhood.

Kesby, Mike. 2005. "Retheorizing Empowerment-through-Participation as a Performance in Space: Beyond Tyranny to Transformation." *Signs: Journal of Women in Culture and Society* 30 (4): 2037–65. https://doi.org/10.1086/428422.

Keyßer, Lorenz T., and Manfred Lenzen. 2021. "1.5 C Degrowth Scenarios Suggest the Need for New Mitigation Pathways." *Nature Communications* 12 (1): 1–16.

Kiss, Bernadett, Filka Sekulova, and Panagiota Kotsila. 2019. "International Comparison of Nature-Based Solutions: Project Report."

Kleinfelder. n.d. "Coastal Resilience Solutions for East Boston and Charlestown." www.kleinfelder.com/project/coastal-resilience-solutions-for-east-boston-and-charlestown/.

Korkmaz, Cansu, and Osman Balaban. 2020. "Sustainability of Urban Regeneration in Turkey: Assessing the Performance of the North Ankara Urban Regeneration Project." *Habitat International* 95: 102081.

Kotsila, Panagiota, Isabelle Anguelovski, Francesc Baró, Johannes Langemeyer, Filka Sekulova, and James J. T. Connolly. 2021. "Nature-Based Solutions as Discursive Tools and Contested Practices in Urban Nature's Neoliberalisation Processes." *Environment and Planning E: Nature and Space* 4 (2): 252–74.

Kotsila, Panagiota, Kathrin Hörschelmann, Isabelle Anguelovski, Filka Sekulova, and Yuliana Lazova. 2020. "Clashing Temporalities of Care and Support as Key Determinants of Transformatory and Justice Potentials in Urban Gardens." *Cities* 106: 102865.

Kotsila, Panagiota, Emilia Oscilowicz, Filka Sekulova, Margarita Triguero-Mas, Isabelle Anguelovski, and Jordi Honey-Rosés. 2021. "Barcelona's Greening Paradox as an Emerging Global City and Tourism Destination." In *The Green City and Social Injustice: 21 Tales from North America and Europe*, edited by Isabelle Anguelovski and James J. T. Connolly, 213–24. London: Routledge.

Kotsila, Panagiota, and V. Subramanian Saravanan. 2017. "Biopolitics Gone to Shit? State Narratives versus Everyday Realities of Water and Sanitation in the Mekong Delta." *World Development* 93: 374–88.

Krähmer, Karl. 2021. "Are Green Cities Sustainable? A Degrowth Critique of Sustainable Urban Development in Copenhagen." *European Planning Studies* 29 (7): 1272–89.

Kronenberg, Jakub, Annegret Haase, Edyta Łaszkiewicz, Attila Antal, Aliaksandra Baravikova, Magdalena Biernacka, Diana Dushkova, et al. 2020. "Environmental Justice in the Context of Urban Green Space Availability, Accessibility, and Attractiveness in Postsocialist Cities." *Cities* 106: 102862. https://doi.org/10.1016/j.cities.2020.102862.

Laín, B., S. Riutort, and A. Julià. 2019. "The B-MINCOME Project. Municipal Innovation on Guaranteed Minimum Incomes and Active Social Policies." *Bhabha Atomic Research Centre Society* 23: 1–18.

Lancee, Bram, and Herman G. Van de Werfhorst. 2012. "Income Inequality and Participation: A Comparison of 24 European Countries." *Social Science Research* 41 (5): 1166–78.

Lefebvre, Henri. 2003. *The Urban Revolution*. Minneapolis, MN: University of Minnesota Press.

Leitner, Helga, Jamie Peck, and Eric S. Sheppard. 2007. *Contesting Neoliberalism: Urban Frontiers*. New York City: Guilford Press.

Lewis, J. O., S. N. Hógáin, and A. Borghi. 2013. "Building Energy Efficiency in European Cities-URBACT II Capitalisation." *Urbact Ii*: 1–52.

Li, Han, Yehua Dennis Wei, and Kim Korinek. 2018. "Modelling Urban Expansion in the Transitional Greater Mekong Region." *Urban Studies* 55 (8): 1729–48.

Linander, Ida, Isabel Goicolea, Erika Alm, Anne Hammarström, and Lisa Harryson. 2019. "(Un) Safe Spaces, Affective Labour and Perceived Health Among People With Trans Experiences Living in Sweden." *Culture, Health & Sexuality* 21 (8): 914–28.

Lombardi Rachel, D., Libby Porter, Austin Barber, and Chris D. F. Rogers. 2011. "Conceptualising Sustainability in UK Urban Regeneration: A Discursive Formation." *Urban Studies* 48 (2): 273–96.

Maantay, Juliana. 2013. "The Collapse of Place: Derelict Land, Deprivation, and Health Inequality in Glasgow, Scotland." *Cities and the Environment (CATE)* 6 (1).

Maantay, Juliana, and Andrew Maroko. 2018. "Brownfields to Greenfields: Environmental Justice Versus Environmental Gentrification." *International Journal of Environmental Research and Public Health* 15 (10): 2233.

MacGregor, Sherilyn, Catherine Walker, and Tally Katz-Gerro. 2019. "'It's What I've Always Done': Continuity and Change in the Household Sustainability Practices of Somali Immigrants in the UK." *Geoforum* 107: 143–53.

Maier, Carolin, Theresia Lindner, and Georg Winkel. 2014. "Stakeholders' Perceptions of Participation in Forest Policy: A Case Study from Baden-Württemberg." *Land Use Policy* 39: 166–76. https://doi.org/10.1016/j.landusepol.2014.02.018.

Matheney, Austin, Carmen Pérez del Pulgar, and Galia Shokry. 2021. "A Green Capital for All?: Austerity, Inequalities and Green Space in Bristol." In *The Green City and Social Injustice: 21 Tales From North America and Europe*, edited by Anguelovski Isabelle and James J. T. Connolly, 49–60. London: Routledge.

McCarthy, James. 2015. "A Socioecological Fix to Capitalist Crisis and Climate Change? The Possibilities and Limits of Renewable Energy." *Environment and Planning A* 47 (12): 2485–502.

McCarthy, James, and Scott Prudham. 2004. "Neoliberal Nature and the Nature of Neoliberalism." *Geoforum* 35 (3): 275–83.

McClintock, Nathan. 2011. "From Industrial Garden to Food Desert." In *Cultivating Food Justice: Race, Class, and Sustainability*, edited by Alison Hope Alkon and Julian Agyeman, 89–120. Cambridge: MIT Press.

McLafferty, Sara, and Valerie Preston. 1992. "Spatial Mismatch and Labor Market Segmentation for African-American and Latina Women." *Economic Geography* 68 (4): 406–31.

McNeill, Donald. 1999. *Urban Change and the European Left: Tales From the New Barcelona*. London: Routledge.

Mies, Maria. 2014. *Patriarchy and Accumulation on a World Scale: Women in the International Division of Labour*. New York: Bloomsbury Publishing.

Miller, Byron. 2015. "Sustainability for Whom? Sustainability How?" In *The Politics of the Urban Sustainability Concept*, edited by David Wilson, 107–16. Champaign, IL: Common Ground.

Mitchell, Bruce, and Juan Franco. 2018. "HOLC 'Redlining' Maps: The Persistent Structure of Segregation and Economic Inequality." *National Community Reinvestment Coalition*, March 20. https://ncrc.org/holc/.

Mohai, Paul, and Robin Saha. 2015. "Which Came First, People or Pollution? A Review of Theory and Evidence from Longitudinal Environmental Justice Studies." *Environmental Research Letters* 10 (12): 125011.

Molotch, Harvey. 1976. "The City as a Growth Machine: Toward a Political Economy of Place." *American Journal of Sociology* 82 (2): 309–32.

Moor, Joost de. 2018. "The 'Efficacy Dilemma' of Transnational Climate Activism: The Case of COP21." *Environmental Politics* 27 (6): 1079–100. https://doi.org/10.1080/09644016.2017.1410315.

Moore-Cherry, Niamh, and Christine Bonnin. 2020. "Playing With Time in Moore Street, Dublin: Urban Redevelopment, Temporal Politics and the Governance of Space-Time." *Urban Geography* 41 (9): 1198–217.

Moore, Darnell L. 2014. "The Price of Blackness: From Ferguson to Bed-Stuy." *The Feminist Wire*, September 4. www.thefeministwire.com/2014/09/price-blackness-ferguson-bed-stuy/.

Morello-Frosch, Rachel, Manuel Pastor, and James Sadd. 2001. "Environmental Justice and Southern California's 'Riskscape' the Distribution of Air Toxics Exposures and Health Risks among Diverse Communities." *Urban Affairs Review* 36 (4): 551–78.

Morning, Ann. 2014. "And You Thought We Had Moved Beyond All That: Biological Race Returns to the Social Sciences." *Ethnic and Racial Studies* 37 (10): 1676–85. https://doi.org/10.1080/01419870.2014.931992.

Morrow, Oona. 2019. "Sharing Food and Risk in Berlin's Urban Food Commons." *Geoforum* 99: 202–12. https://doi.org/10.1016/j.geoforum.2018.09.003.

Mosthaf, Alexander, Thorsten Schank, and Claus Schnabel. 2014. "Low-Wage Employment versus Unemployment: Which One Provides Better Prospects for Women?" *IZA Journal of European Labor Studies* 3 (1): 1–17.

Neo, Harvey, and C. P. Pow. 2015. "Eco-Cities and the Promise of Socio-Environmental Justice." In *The International Handbook of Political Ecology*, edited by Raymond L. Bryant. Cheltenham and Northampton, MA: Edward Elgar Publishing.

Nussbaum, Martha Craven. 2000. "Women's Capabilities and Social Justice." *Journal of Human Development* 1 (2): 219–47.

Nussbaum, Martha Craven. 2006. *Frontiers of Justice: Disability, Nationality, Species Membership*. Cambridge, MA: Belknap Press.

Oscilowicz, Emilia, Jordi Honey-Rosés, Isabelle Anguelovski, Margarita Triguero-Mas, and Helen Cole. 2020. "Young Families and Children in Gentrifying Neighbourhoods: How Gentrification Reshapes Use and Perception of Green Play Spaces." *Local Environment* 25 (10): 765–86.

Oseland, Stina Ellevseth. 2019. "Breaking Silos: Can Cities Break down Institutional Barriers in Climate Planning?" *Journal of Environmental Policy & Planning* 21 (4): 345–57.

Pascual-Molinas, Nuria, and Ramon Ribera-Fumaz. 2013. "Retail gentrification in Ciutat Vella, Barcelona." In *Whose Urban Renaissance? An International Comparison of Urban Regeneration Strategies*, edited by Libby Porter and Kate Shaw, 180–90. London: Routledge.

Park, Lisa Sun-Hee, and David Pellow. 2011. *The Slums of Aspen*. New York: New York University Press.

Partidario, Maria Rosario, and William R. Sheate. 2013. "Knowledge Brokerage-Potential for Increased Capacities and Shared Power in Impact Assessment." *Environmental Impact Assessment Review* 39: 26–36.

Paulson, Susan, Giacomo D'Alisa, Federico Demaria, and Giorgos Kallis. 2020. *The Case for Degrowth*. Cambridge, Oxford, and Boston: John Wiley & Sons.

Pearsall, Hamil, and Isabelle Anguelovski. 2016. "Contesting and Resisting Environmental Gentrification: Responses to New Paradoxes and Challenges for Urban Environmental Justice." *Sociological Research Online* 21 (3): 1–7.

Pearsall, Hamil, and Joseph Pierce. 2010. "Urban Sustainability and Environmental Justice: Evaluating the Linkages in Public Planning/Policy Discourse." *Local Environment* 15 (6): 569–80.

Pearson, Natalie. 2019. "The Taxes That Sent Vancouver's Luxury Housing Market Reeling." *Bloomberg.com*, April 16. www.bloomberg.com/news/articles/2019-04-16/the-taxes-that-sent-vancouver-s-luxury-housing-marketreeling.

Peck, Jamie, and Adam Tickell. 2002. "Neoliberalizing Space." *Antipode* 34 (3): 380–404.

Pellow, David N. 2016. "Toward a Critical Environmental Justice Studies: Black Lives Matter as an Environmental Justice Challenge." *Du Bois Review: Social Science Research on Race* 13 (2): 221–36.

Pérez del Pulgar, Carmen. 2021. "Dismantling the Just City: The Unevenness of Green Experiences in Amsterdam Noord." In *The Green City and Social Injustice: 21 Tales from North America and Europe*, edited by Isabelle Anguelovski and James J. T. Connolly, 35–48. London: Routledge.

Pérez-del-Pulgar, Carmen, Isabelle Anguelovski, Helen V. S. Cole, Jeroen de Bont, James Connolly, Francesc Baró, Yesika Díaz, Mario Fontán-Vela, Talita Duarte-Salles, and Margarita Triguero-Mas. 2021. "The Relationship Between Residential Proximity to Outdoor Play Spaces and Children's Mental and Behavioral Health: The Importance of Neighborhood Socio-Economic Characteristics." *Environmental Research*: 111326.

Perkins, Harold A. 2009. "Out From the (Green) Shadow? Neoliberal Hegemony through the Market Logic of Shared Urban Environmental Governance." *Political Geography* 28 (7): 395–405.

———. 2011. "Gramsci in Green: Neoliberal Hegemony Through Urban Forestry and the Potential for a Political Ecology of Praxis." *Geoforum* 42 (5): 558–66.

Pickett, Kate, and Richard Wilkinson. 2010. *The Spirit Level: Why Equality Is Better for Everyone*. London: Penguin.

Pierre, Jon. 2011. *The Politics of Urban Governance*. London: Macmillan International Higher Education.

Poe, J., and J. Bellamy. 2020. "Plantation Urbanism: Legacy, Property and Policing in Louisville, Kentucky." *Radical Housing Journal* 2 (2): 143–64.

Poethig, Erika C. Solomon Greene, Christina Plerhoples Stacy, Tanaya Srini, and Brady Meixell. 2018. *Inclusive Recovery in US Cities*. Washington, DC: Urban Institute. Accessed March 16, 2022. www.urban.org/research/publication/inclusive-recovery-us-cities.

Porter, Libby, and Kate Shaw. 2013. *Whose Urban Renaissance? An International Comparison of Urban Regeneration Strategies*. London: Routledge.

Pretty, Jules N. 1995. "Participatory Learning for Sustainable Agriculture." *World Development* 23 (8): 1247–63. https://doi.org/10.1016/0305-750X(95)00046-F.

Privitera, Elisa, Marco Armiero, and Filippo Gravagno. 2021. "Seeking Justice in Risk Landscapes. Small Data and Toxic Autobiographies from an Italian Petrochemical Town (Gela, Sicily)." *Local Environment*: 1–25.

Pulido, Laura. 2000. "Rethinking Environmental Racism: White Privilege and Urban Development in Southern California." *Annals of the Association of American Geographers* 90 (1): 12–40. https://doi.org/10.1111/0004-5608.00182.

———. 2008. "Rethinking Environmental Racism: White Privilege and Urban Development in Southern California." In *Environment: Critical Essays in Human Geography* (1st ed.), edited by K. Anderson and B. Braun, 379–407. London: Routledge.

Pulido, Laura, and Juan De Lara. 2018. "Reimagining 'Justice' in Environmental Justice: Radical Ecologies, Decolonial Thought, and the Black Radical Tradition." *Environment and Planning E: Nature and Space* 1 (1–2): 76–98.

Puskás, Nikolett, Yaser Abunnasr, and Salpy Naalbandian. 2021. "Assessing Deeper Levels of Participation in Nature-Based Solutions in Urban Landscapes—A Literature Review of Real-World Cases." *Landscape and Urban Planning* 210: 104065. https://doi.org/https://doi.org/10.1016/j.landurbplan.2021.104065.

Ranganathan, Malini, and Eve Bratman. 2021. "From Urban Resilience to Abolitionist Climate Justice in Washington, DC." *Antipode* 53 (1): 115–37.

Rigolon, Alessandro, Matthew Browning, and Viniece Jennings. 2018. "Inequities in the Quality of Urban Park Systems: An Environmental Justice Investigation of Cities in the United States." *Landscape and Urban Planning* 178: 156–69.

Rittel, Horst W. J., and Melvin M. Webber. 1973. "Dilemmas in a General Theory of Planning." *Policy Sciences* 4 (2): 155–69.

Robinson, J. 2005. *Ordinary Cities: Between Modernity and Development*. 1st ed. London: Routledge.

Romanello, Marina, Alice McGushin, Claudia Di Napoli, Paul Drummond, Nick Hughes, Louis Jamart, Harry Kennard, Pete Lampard, Baltazar Solano Rodriguez, and Nigel Arnell. 2021. "The 2021 Report of the Lancet Countdown on Health and Climate Change: Code Red for a Healthy Future." *The Lancet* 398 (10311): 1619–62.

Root Cause Research Center. 2021. "Property and Policing in Louisville, KY: A Spatial Analysis of Nuisance Law, Redevelopment, Personhood, and Police Violence." November 19. https://storymaps.arcgis.com/stories/4add4e9971c44b7e80d20d22671b6973.

Rosa, Salvatore Paolo De. 2018. "A Political Geography of 'Waste Wars' in Campania (Italy): Competing Territorialisations and Socio-Environmental Conflicts." *Political Geography* 67: 46–55.

Rosol, Marit. 2012. "Community Volunteering as Neoliberal Strategy? Green Space Production in Berlin." *Antipode* 44 (1): 239–57.

———. 2013. "Vancouver's 'EcoDensity' Planning Initiative: A Struggle over Hegemony?" *Urban Studies* 50 (11): 2238–55.

Rouse, Cecilia, Jared Bernstein, Helen Knudsen, and Jefferey Zhang. 2021. "Exclusionary Zoning: Its Effect on Racial Discrimination in the Housing Market." *The White House*, June 17. www.whitehouse.gov/cea/blog/2021/06/17/exclusionary-zoning-its-effect-on-racial-discrimination-in-the-housing-market/.

Roy, Ananya. 2011. "Slumdog Cities: Rethinking Subaltern Urbanism." *International Journal of Urban and Regional Research* 35 (2): 223–38. https://doi.org/10.1111/j.1468-2427.2011.01051.x.

Ryan, Denise. 2016. "The $31b 'Green Branding' of Vancouver." January 28. https://vancouversun.com/news/metro/the-31b-green-branding-of-vancouver.

Ryneveld, Tara van. 2021. "The Digital Divide as 'Smart' City Inequality." *Undisciplined Environments*. Accessed March 15 2020. https://undisciplinedenviron ments.org/2021/03/11/the-digital-divide-as-smart-city-inequality/

Safransky, Sara. 2014. "Greening the Urban Frontier: Race, Property, and Resettlement in Detroit." *Geoforum* 56: 237–48. https://doi.org/10.1016/j.geoforum. 2014.06.003.

Salleh, Ariel. 2009. *Eco-Sufficiency & Global Justice: Women Write Political Ecology*. London: Pluto Press.

Samara, Tony Roshan. 2010. "Policing Development: Urban Renewal as Neo-Liberal Security Strategy." *Urban Studies* 47 (1): 197–214. https://doi.org/10.1177/0042098009349772.

Sareen, Siddharth, Devyn Remme, Katinka Wågsæther, and Håvard Haarstad. 2021. "A Matter of Time: Explicating Temporality in Science and Technology Studies and Bergen's Car-Free Zone Development." *Energy Research & Social Science* 78: 102128.

Säumel, Ina, Suhana Reddy, and Thomas Wachtel. 2019. "Edible City Solutions— One Step Further to Foster Social Resilience Through Enhanced Socio-Cultural Ecosystem Services in Cities." *Sustainability* 11 (4): 972. https://doi.org/10.3390/su11040972.

Scheidel, Arnim, Daniela Del Bene, Juan Liu, Grettel Navas, Sara Mingorría, Federico Demaria, Sofia Avila, Brototi Roy, Irmak Ertör, and Leah Temper. 2020. "Environmental Conflicts and Defenders: A Global Overview." *Global Environmental Change* 63: 102104.

Scherhaufer, Patrick, Philipp Klittich, and Aron Buzogány. 2021. "Between Illegal Protests and Legitimate Resistance. Civil Disobedience against Energy Infrastructures." *Utilities Policy* 72: 101249. https://doi.org/https://doi.org/10.1016/j.jup.2021.101249.

Schlosberg, David. 2013. "Theorising Environmental Justice: The Expanding Sphere of a Discourse." *Environmental Politics* 22 (1): 37–55.

Schmelzer, Matthias. 2015. "The Growth Paradigm: History, Hegemony, and the Contested Making of Economic Growthmanship." *Ecological Economics* 118: 262–71.

Schneider, Annemarie, Chaoyi Chang, and Kurt Paulsen. 2015. "The Changing Spatial Form of Cities in Western China." *Landscape and Urban Planning* 135: 40–61.

Scott, Alister. 2011. "Focussing in on Focus Groups: Effective Participative Tools or Cheap Fixes for Land Use Policy?" *Land Use Policy* 28 (4): 684–94. https://doi.org/10.1016/j.landusepol.2010.12.004.

Sekulova, F., I. Anguelovski, L. Arguelles, S. Becker, A. Prampolini, F. Martellozzo, C. Hendrickson, A. Fischer, L. Dinnie, A. Pinker, P. Revell, J. Msika, O. Virkkula, T. Kahkonen, J. Pihlajamaa, and C. Nastase. 2016a. "Analysis of Qualitative

Success Factors for Community-based Initiatives." A Scientific Report of the TESS FP7 Research Project.

Sekulova, F., I. Anguelovski, L. Arguelles, S. Becker, A. Prampolini, F. Martellozzo, C. Hendrickson, A. Fischer, L. Dinnie, A. Pinker, P. Revell, J. Msika, O. Virkkula, T. Kahkonen, J. Pihlajamaa, and C. Nastase. 2016b. "Success Factors for Community-based Initiatives: Summary Report on Case Study Findings." A Scientific Report of the TESS FP7 Research Project.

Sekulova, F., Isabelle Anguelovski, Lucia Argüelles, and Joana Conill. 2017. "A 'Fertile Soil' for Sustainability-Related Community Initiatives: A New Analytical Framework." *Environment and Planning A* 49 (10): 2362–82.

Sekulova, F., I. Anguelovski, B. Kiss, P. Kotsila, Francesc Baró, Yuliya Voytenko Palgan, and James Connolly. 2021a. "The Governance of Nature-Based Solutions in the City at the Intersection of Justice and Equity." *Cities* 112. https://doi.org/10.1016/j.cities.2021.103136.

Sekulova, Filka, Isabelle Anguelovski, Bernadett Kiss, Panagiota Kotsila, Francesc Baró, Yuliya Voytenko Palgan, and James Connolly. 2021b. "The Governance of Nature-Based Solutions in the City at the Intersection of Justice and Equity." *Cities* 112: 103136.

Sekulova, Filka, Giorgos Kallis, and François Schneider. 2017. "Climate Change, Happiness and Income from a Degrowth Perspective." *Handbook on Growth and Sustainability* 160.

Sen, Amartya. 2000. *Development as Freedom* (Reprint Edition). New York: Anchor.

Seto, Karen C., Burak Güneralp, and Lucy R. Hutyra. 2012. "Global Forecasts of Urban Expansion to 2030 and Direct Impacts on Biodiversity and Carbon Pools." *Proceedings of the National Academy of Sciences* 109 (40): 16083–88.

Seyle, D. Conor, and Matthew Wilburn King. 2014. "Understanding Governance." In *State of the World 2014*, edited by The Worldwatch Institute, 20–28. Washington, DC: Island Press.

SHARECITY. 2019. "Q&A with Anna Davies, Project Lead for the SHARECITY Project." September 30. https://sharecity.ie/q-and-a-anna-davies/.

Shi, Linda, Eric Chu, Isabelle Anguelovski, Alexander Aylett, Jessica Debats, Kian Goh, Todd Schenk, Karen C. Seto, David Dodman, and Debra Roberts. 2016. "Roadmap towards Justice in Urban Climate Adaptation Research." *Nature Climate Change* 6 (2): 131.

Shokry, Galia, Isabelle Anguelovski, James J. T. Connolly, Andrew Maroko, and Hamil Pearsall. 2022. "'They Didn't See It Coming': Green Resilience Planning and Vulnerability to Future Climate Gentrification." *Housing Policy Debate* 32 (1): 211–45.

Shokry, Galia, James J. T. Connolly, and Isabelle Anguelovski. 2020. "Understanding Climate Gentrification and Shifting Landscapes of Protection and Vulnerability in Green Resilient Philadelphia." *Urban Climate* 31 (March): 100539. https://doi.org/10.1016/j.uclim.2019.100539.

Simpson, Michael, and Jen Bagelman. 2018. "Decolonizing Urban Political Ecologies: The Production of Nature in Settler Colonial Cities." *Annals of the American Association of Geographers* 108 (2): 558–68. https://doi.org/10.1080/24694452.2017.1392285.

Smith, Neil. 1996. *The New Urban Frontier: Gentrification and the Revanchist City*. London: Routledge.

———. 2010. *Uneven Development: Nature, Capital, and the Production of Space*. Georgia: University of Georgia Press.

Soederberg, Susanne, and Alan Walks. "Producing and Governing Inequalities Under Planetary Urbanization: From Urban Age to Urban Revolution?" *Geoforum* 89 (2017): 107–13.

Solomon, Danyelle, Connor Maxwell, and Abril Castro. 2019. "Systemic Inequality: Displacement, Exclusion, and Segregation: How America's Housing System Undermines Wealth Building in Communities of Color." *Center for American Progress*, August 7. www.americanprogress.org/article/systemic-inequality-displacement-exclusion-segregation/.

Sovacool, Benjamin K., Björn-Ola Linnér, and Michael E. Goodsite. 2015. "The Political Economy of Climate Adaptation." *Nature Climate Change* 5 (7): 616–18.

Squires, Gregory D., and Frank Woodruff. 2019. "Redlining." In *The Wiley Blackwell Encyclopedia of Urban and Regional Studies*. Major Reference Works. https://doi.org/10.1002/9781118568446.eurs0260.

Stavrides, Stavros. 2020. "Common Spaces of Urban Emancipation." In *Common Spaces of Urban Emancipation*. Manchester: Manchester University Press.

Stovall, Maya. 2019. "'It's the' Hood. But That Means It's Home!": African American Feminist Critical Geographic Wanderings in the Anthropology of Space and Place." *Transforming Anthropology* 27 (1): 50–67. https:///10.1111/traa.12142.

Sullivan, Daniel Monroe. 2014. "From Food Desert to Food Mirage: Race, Social Class, and Food Shopping in a Gentrifying Neighborhood." *Advances in Applied Sociology* 4: 30–5. doi: 10.4236/aasoci.2014.41006.

Sun, Liqun, Ji Chen, Qinglan Li, and Dian Huang. 2020. "Dramatic Uneven Urbanization of Large Cities Throughout the World in Recent Decades." *Nature Communications* 11 (1): 1–9.

Swyngedouw, Erik. 1997. "Neither Global Nor Local: 'Glocalization' and the Politics of Scale." In *Spaces of Globalization: Reasserting the Power of the Local*, edited by Kevin Cox, 137–66. New York: Guilford Press.

———. 2005. "Governance Innovation and the Citizen: The Janus Face of Governance-beyond-the-State." *Urban Studies* 42 (11): 1991–2006.

———. 2007. "Impossible 'Sustainability' and the Postpolitical Condition." In *The Sustainable Development Paradox: Urban Political Economy in the United States and Europe*, edited by David Gibbs and Rob Krueger, 13–40. New York: Guilford Press.

———. 2014. "Losing Our Fear! Facing the Anthro-Obscene*." Undisciplined Environments. 2014. https://undisciplinedenvironments.org/2014/10/20/losing-our-fear-facing-the-anthro-obscene/.

Swyngedouw, Erik, Frank Moulaert, and Arantxa Rodriguez. 2002. "Neoliberal Urbanization in Europe: Large—Scale Urban Development Projects and the New Urban Policy." *Antipode* 34 (3): 542–77.

Szaboova, Lucy, Ricardo Safra de Campos, W. Neil Adger, Mumuni Abu, Samuel Nii Ardey Codjoe, Maria Franco Gavonel, Shouvik Das, Tasneem Siddiqui, Mahmudol Hassan Rocky, and Sugata Hazra. 2022. "Urban Sustainability and the Subjective Well-being of Migrants: The Role of Risks, Place Attachment, and Aspirations." *Population, Space and Place* 28 (1): e2505.

Tammaru, Tiit, Szymon Marcin´czak, Raivo Aunap, Maarten van Ham, and Heleen Janssen. 2020. "Relationship between Income Inequality and Residential Segregation of Socioeconomic Groups." *Regional Studies* 54 (4): 450–61. https://doi. org/10.1080/00343404.2018.1540035.

Taylor, Dorceta. 2014. *Toxic Communities: Environmental Racism, Industrial Pollution, and Residential Mobility.* New York City: New York University Press.

Thomson, Harriet, Carolyn Snell, and Stefan Bouzarovski. 2017. "Health, Well-Being and Energy Poverty in Europe: A Comparative Study of 32 European Countries." *International Journal of Environmental Research and Public Health* 14 (6): 584. https://doi.org/10.3390/ijerph14060584.

Thompson, Matthew. 2021. "What's so New About New Municipalism?" *Progress in Human Geography* 45 (2): 317–42.

Toxopeus, Helen, Panagiota Kotsila, Marta Conde, Attila Katona, Alexander P. N. van der Jagt, and Friedemann Polzin. 2020. "How 'Just' Is Hybrid Governance of Urban Nature-Based Solutions?" *Cities* 105: 102839. https://doi.org/10.1016/j. cities.2020.102839.

Trencher, Gregory, Masaru Yarime, Kes B. McCormick, Christopher N. H. Doll, and Steven B. Kraines. 2013. "Beyond the Third Mission: Exploring the Emerging University Function of Co-Creation for Sustainability." *Science and Public Policy* 41 (2): 151–79. https://doi.org/10.1093/scipol/sct044.

Triguero-Mas, Margarita, Isabelle Anguelovski, Melissa García-Lamarca, Lucía Argüelles, Carmen Perez-del-Pulgar, Galia Shokry, James J. T. Connolly, and Helen V. S. Cole. 2021. "Natural Outdoor Environments' Health Effects in Gentrifying Neighborhoods: Disruptive Green Landscapes for Underprivileged Neighborhood Residents." *Social Science & Medicine* 279: 113964.

Triguero-Mas, Margarita, Payam Dadvand, Marta Cirach, David Martínez, Antonia Medina, Anna Mompart, Xavier Basagaña, Regina Gražulevičienė, and Mark J. Nieuwenhuijsen. 2015. "Natural Outdoor Environments and Mental and Physical Health: Relationships and Mechanisms." *Environment International* 77: 35–41.

Truelove, Yaffa. 2011. "(Re-)Conceptualizing Water Inequality in Delhi, India Through a Feminist Political Ecology Framework." *Geoforum* 42 (2): 143–52. https://doi.org/10.1016/j.geoforum.2011.01.004.

Truelove, Yaffa, and Hanna A. Ruszczyk. 2022. "Bodies as Urban Infrastructure: Gender, Intimate Infrastructures and Slow Infrastructural Violence." *Political Geography* 92: 102492. https://doi.org/10.1016/j.polgeo.2021.102492.

Tulloch, Lynley, and David Neilson. 2014. "The Neoliberalisation of Sustainability." *Citizenship, Social and Economics Education* 13 (1): 26–38.

UN. 2015. *Transforming Our World: The 2030 Agenda for Sustainable Development.* New York. http://bit.ly/TransformAgendaSDG-pdf.

UN Habitat. 2002. *The Global Campaign on Urban Governance.* Concept paper. 2nd ed., March. https://unhabitat.org/sites/default/files/download-manager-files/ Global Campaign on Urban Governance.pdf.

UNDESA. 2020. "World Social Report 2020: Inequality in a Rapidly Changing World." www.un.org/development/desa/dspd/wp-content/uploads/sites/22/2020/ 02/World-Social-Report2020-FullReport.pdf.

UrbanTurf. 2020. "Rising Prices Don't Dampen Sales: The Anacostia Housing Market, By the Numbers." *Urban Turf,* August 3, 2020. https://dc.urbanturf.com/

articles/blog/rising-prices-dont-dampen-sales-the-anacostia-housing-market-by-the-numbers/17145.

Vale, Lawrence J. 2013. *Purging the Poorest: Public Housing and the Design Politics of Twice-Cleared Communities*. Chicago: University of Chicago Press.

Valli, Chiara. 2015. "A Sense of Displacement: Long-Time Residents' Feelings of Displacement in Gentrifying Bushwick, New York." *International Journal of Urban and Regional Research* 39 (6): 1191–208.

Velden, Maja van der. 2004. "From Communities of Practice to Communities of Resistance: Civil Society and Cognitive Justice." *Development* 47 (1): 73–80. https://doi.org/10.1057/palgrave.development.1100004.

Venter, Zander S., Charlie M. Shackleton, Francini Van Staden, Odirilwe Selomane, and Vanessa A. Masterson. 2020. "Green Apartheid: Urban Green Infrastructure Remains Unequally Distributed across Income and Race Geographies in South Africa." *Landscape and Urban Planning* 203: 103889. https://doi.org/https://doi.org/10.1016/j.landurbplan.2020.103889.

Wacquant, Loïc. 2014. "Marginality, Ethnicity and Penalty in the Neo-Liberal City: An Analytic Cartography." *Ethnic and Racial Studies* 37 (10): 1687–711. https://doi.org/10.1080/01419870.2014.931991.

Wang, Xiaoxiao, Ruiting Shi, and Ying Zhou. 2020. "Dynamics of Urban Sprawl and Sustainable Development in China." *Socio-Economic Planning Sciences* 70: 100736.

Warlenius, Rikard, Gregory Pierce, and Vasna Ramasar. 2015. "Reversing the Arrow of Arrears: The Concept of 'Ecological Debt' and Its Value for Environmental Justice." *Global Environmental Change* 30: 21–30.

Wascher, Dirk, Maya Kneafsey, Marina Pintar, and Annette Piorr. 2015. *FOODMETRES: Food Planning and Innovation for Sustainable Metropolitan Regions Synthesis Report 2015*. Wageningen, UR: FOODMETRES.

Webber, Sophie, Sara Nelson, Nate Millington, Gareth Bryant, and Patrick Bigger. 2022. "Financing Reparative Climate Infrastructures: Capital Switching, Repair, and Decommodification." *Antipode* 54 (3): 934–58.

Wei, Yehua Dennis. 2015. "Zone Fever, Project Fever: Development Policy, Economic Transition, and Urban Expansion in China." *Geographical Review* 105 (2): 156–77.

Wei, Yehua Dennis, and Reid Ewing. 2018. "Urban Expansion, Sprawl and Inequality." *Landscape and Urban Planning* 177: 259–65.

Westman, Linda, and Vanesa Castán Broto. 2022. "Urban Transformations to Keep All the Same: The Power of Ivy Discourses." *Antipode* 54 (4): 1320–43.

While, Aidan, Andrew E. G. Jonas, and David Gibbs. 2004. "The Environment and the Entrepreneurial City: Searching for the Urban 'Sustainability Fix' in Manchester and Leeds." *International Journal of Urban and Regional Research* 28 (3): 549–69.

White, Sarah C. 1996. "Depoliticising Development: The Uses and Abuses of Participation." *Development in Practice* 6 (1): 6–15. https://doi.org/10.1080/0961452961000157564.

Wiig, Alan. 2018. "Secure the City, Revitalize the Zone: Smart Urbanization in Camden, New Jersey." *Environment and Planning C: Politics and Space* 36 (3): 403–22.

Wilker, Jost, Karsten Rusche, and Christine Rymsa-Fitschen. 2016. "Improving Participation in Green Infrastructure Planning." *Planning Practice & Research* 31 (3): 229–49. https://doi.org/10.1080/02697459.2016.1158065.

Williams, David R., and Chiquita Collins. 2016. "Racial Residential Segregation: A Fundamental Cause of Racial Disparities in Health." *Public Health Reports* 116 (5): 404–16.

Williams, David R., Michelle Sternthal, and Rosalind J. Wright. 2009. "Social Determinants: Taking the Social Context of Asthma Seriously." *Pediatrics* 123 (Supplement 3): S174–84.

Wilson, David. 2015a. "Introduction: The Rise of Urban Sustainability and This Book." In *The Politics of the Urban Sustainability Concept*, edited by David Wilson, 1–7. Champaign: Common Ground Publishing.

———. 2015b. *The Politics of the Urban Sustainability Concept.* Champaign: Common Ground Publishing.

Wilson, Japhy, and Erik Swyngedouw. 2015. *The Post-Political and Its Discontents: Spaces of Depoliticisation, Spectres of Radical Politics.* Edinburgh: Edinburgh University Press.

Wiltz, Teresa. 2018. "This City Wants to Reverse Segregation by Reviving Neighborhoods." *Pew Charitable Trust*, October 3. www.pewtrusts.org/es/research-and-analysis/blogs/stateline/2018/10/03/this-city-wants-to-reverse-segregation-by-reviving-neighborhoods.

Wüstemann, Henry, Dennis Kalisch, and Jens Kolbe. 2017. "Access to Urban Green Space and Environmental Inequalities in Germany." *Landscape and Urban Planning* 164: 124–31.

Wyly, Elvin K., and Daniel J. Hammel. 1999. "Islands of Decay in Seas of Renewal: Housing Policy and the Resurgence of Gentrification." *Housing Policy Debate* 10 (4): 711–71. https://doi.org/10.1080/10511482.1999.9521348.

Yabanci, Bilge. 2019. "Turkey's Tamed Civil Society: Containment and Appropriation Under a Competitive Authoritarian Regime." *Journal of Civil Society* 15 (4): 285–306. https://doi.org/10.1080/17448689.2019.1668627.

Young, Iris Marion. 2011. *Justice and the Politics of Difference.* Princeton, NJ: Princeton University Press.

Zernike, Kate. 2016. "A Sea of Charter Schools in Detroit Leaves Students Adrift." *New York Times*, June 28. www.nytimes.com/2016/06/29/us/for-detroits-children-more-school-choice-but-not-better-schools.html.

Index

Note: Page numbers in *italics* indicate a figure on the corresponding page.

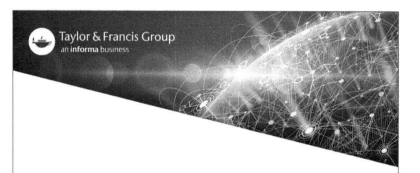